CONFRONTATION IN SPIRITUAL CARE
An Anthology for Clinical Caregivers

by

Gordon J. Hilsman, Author-Editor
Sandra Walker, Co-Editor

Summit Bay Press
Olympia, Washington

CONFRONTATION IN SPIRITUAL CARE:
An Anthology for Clinical Caregivers
Copyright @ 2022 by Gordon J. Hilsman

ISBN: 9798809255783

Printed in the United States of America

All rights reserved. No part of this work may be reproduced or used in any form or by any means—graphic, electronic, or mechanical, including photocopying or information storage or retrieval systems—without written permission from the author.

The scanning, uploading, and distribution of this book or any part thereof via the Internet or any other means without the permission of the author is illegal and punishable by law. Please purchase only authorized editions and do not participate in or encourage the electronic piracy of copyrighted materials.

Gordon Hilsman website: www.SpiritualClinician.com

WHAT PEOPLE ARE SAYING

Confrontation in Spiritual Care, edited by Gordon Hilsman and Sandra Walker, makes a compelling case for the power of confrontation as empathy's indispensable partner in the work of healing and restoring wholeness. The rich chapters in this book written by professionals in the field of spiritual care and healthcare make a convincing case for the growth-inducing power of skillful and compassionate challenge. I found myself drawn in by the rich stories about wise caregivers and mentors challenging their patients or students in life-enhancing ways. The evocative writing moved me to deep appreciation for the tools explored in these pages and for the courageous healers who honed and are now teaching us the art of confrontation for the benefit of those we serve.

Challenging the preconception of seeing confrontation in a negative light as motivated by aggression or anger, the unfolding chapters paint a beautiful picture of the use of skillful confrontation within a caring holding environment and a relationship of trust which gives it its potency and transformative power. Substantial chapters explore the expert use of caring confrontation across cultures, in palliative care conversations, in grief work, addiction treatment, when working with traumatized individuals or combat vets, and a variety of other contexts.

A powerful chapter by Buhuro challenges the motif of the angry black woman and re-images the use of confrontation in the context of empowerment to enhance the lives of those marginalized by oppressive social structures. I came away feeling compassionately but seriously challenged to more deeply incorporate into my work the profound wisdom and rich practices in this book.

I highly recommend this volume to physicians, nurses, mental health professionals, spiritual care providers, pastoral educators, clergy, and other healers.

Jurgen Schwing, MA, ACPE Certified Educator, Director of Spiritual Care, Kaiser Permanente Diablo Service Area, Walnut Creek, CA

Confrontation in Spiritual Care is a necessary and timely collection of perspectives on the topic. The reader will find advice on the "how to confront" as well as on different contexts of care and confrontation. Since David Augsburger's third edition book *Caring Enough to Confront* in 2009, confrontation has increasingly vanished from spiritual care. The editors Gordon Hilsman and Sandra Walker found educational ways of challenging the field with its need to learn and re-learn to better confront in caring ways.

Angelika Zollfrank, ACPE Certified Educator, Harvard University's McLean Psychiatric Hospital, Belmont MA

Gordon Hilsman, longtime chaplain, chaplain educator, and author has masterfully brought together a comprehensive collection of various instances where compassionate confrontation is needed. The chapters—written by Hilsman and other guest authors—looks at general and specific areas of relationships and ministries that would benefit from confrontation. I found each chapter intriguing and insightful, bringing comprehensive and in-depth assessments and intervention styles up to the surface of my comprehension."

Chaplain Dick Cathell, PhD, MDiv, former board member for the Association of Professional Chaplains and author of *The Gift of Becoming: Fulfilling Nine Basic Needs for Enhanced Living,* (Village Press: 2019)

Confrontation in Spiritual Care offers a breadth of situations requiring life-giving confrontation often in situations in which confrontation is particularly scary; for example, those suffering with addictions to alcohol; the mentally ill both in the hospital and on the streets; those who are engaging in racism; veterans suffering from moral injury; professional colleagues, both practitioners and supervisors; congregations when bad behavior hurts community; and God when pain and evil persist. These chapters provide wonderfully vulnerable clinical examples of how to responsibly engage in confrontation. I can't wait for this book to be published so I can own a copy of this incredible resource!

Judith R. Ragsdale, PhD, ACPE Certified Educator, Cincinnati, OH

Confrontation is not something most of us do well. This is often to the detriment of ourselves and those we serve. That is what makes this book a must read. Through my many years of professional involvement with the spiritual care movement in North America, I have been privileged to work with many of its authors. I have experienced and observed first-hand the wisdom, skills, and compassion that are so clearly elucidated in its pages. Whether you are a parish pastor, an educator in the field of spiritual care, or a professional or lay spiritual care practitioner, reading and internalizing the resources found here will be both personally rewarding and skill enhancing.

Rev. Gary W. Sartain, ACPE Educator Emeritus; former Regional Director, North Central Region, ACPE Inc former Regional Coordinator of Chaplaincy Services, Province of Ontario, Canada

---

As a general concept, talking about conflict is a crucial aspect of spiritual care and education. Our field needs practitioners and educators to step up and challenge one another and especially our students by listening to what we agree with and what we do not. In effect, we can only relate and teach authentically when we can allow open and honest conflict.

This book certainly engages us from many theoretical perspectives to do so.

Rabbi Jeffery Silberman, ACPE and NAJC (Neshama) Certified Educator, Westport CT

CONTENTS

DEDICATION xiv

FOREWORD: By The Rev Karen Hutt Certified Clinical Educator Minneapolis MN xv

PREFACE xix

DISCLAIMER PLUS xxiii

ACKNOWLEDGMENTS xxvi

PART ONE: Empathy's Partner: The Enigmatic Nature and Value of Confrontation 1

Chapter One: The Face-to-Face Gateway in Spiritual Care by Gordon J Hilsman 3

    Confrontation as Emotional Reflection 6

    Confrontation as an Interpretation 7

    Confrontation as a Question 7

    Piercing the Music: Finding Your Soul to Midwife 'the New' in Interpersonal Care 14

Chapter Two: The Transforming Potential of Being Confronted by Wes McIntyre 19

PART TWO: Faces of Confrontive Patient Care 27

Chapter Three: The Unconsciously Hidden: Potential Drinking Problems in the General Hospital by Gordon J Hilsman 29

ix

Chapter Four: Confronting Patients and Physician Colleagues in Palliative Care by Juan Iregui and Gordon J. Hilsman 45

    Confronting Patients and Families 47

    Confronting Physicians 52

Chapter Five: God's Hands, Miracles, and the Good Fight by Amy Sanchez 59

Chapter Six: The Previously Traumatized: Confrontation in the Context of Trauma-Informed Care by Rabbi Beth Naditch 67

Chapter Seven: Sapphire Dignified: Resisting the Angry Black Woman Motif in CPE Supervision by The Rev Dr Danielle J Buhuro 79

    The Invention of 'Mammy': White Supremacy's Cultural Production of Evil 81

    Still Desiring Mammy and Despising Sapphire: Labeling Black Women as "Angry" in CPE Group Life and Process 87

    Inviting Confrontation Through an "Empathy-Education-Empowerment" Approach 90

    Sapphire Dignified 92

Chapter Eight: The Confused, Alarmed, and Vulnerable: Mental Health and Psychiatry by Randy Meyers 99

    Melody, Alice and Kammy 101

    Lil Wayne 105

    Eric and Sam 113

Chapter Nine: The Core-Shaken: Confronting Moral Injury with Combat Veterans in Groups by Chaplain Gregory J Widmer 123

Define Moral Injury 124

Describing Moral Reintegration 127

Confrontation of In-Treatment Combat Veterans with Moral Injury 130

Confrontation through Symbols 130

Confrontation through Provocation 131

Confrontation through Community 133

Spiritual Care for Combat Veterans as Patients in a General Hospital 134

Chapter Ten: Confrontation When Words Fail by Joel C Graves 139

Chapter Eleven: The Unsheltered Wanderer by Rod Seeger with Gordon J Hilsman 147

Becoming Courageous, Comfortable and Skilled with Confronting 149

Confronting a Person Whose Perception of a Situation has Dangerously Broken with Reality 150

Confronting a Person Who is a Danger to Self 151

Confronting a Person Hurting Another 152

Confronting a Person Making Disturbances and Being Distracting 153

Confronting a Person Blatantly Manipulating in Ridicule of a Minor Authority 153

Chapter Twelve: The Bereft: Beckoning Forth the Grief by Fr John Bucchino 157

Chapter Thirteen: The Dying: Confronting as a Tool in End-of-Life Spiritual Care by The Rev Timothy Shipe, MDiv, BCC 165

   Confronting Patients 167

   Confronting Families 171

   Confronting Interdisciplinary Care Team Colleagues 174

PART THREE: Confronting in Professional Practice 179

Chapter Fourteen: How to Confront Your Organizational Superior by Jill Rasmussen-Baker 181

   Foundations: Building Trust and Rapport 182

   Confrontation About Staffing: My Three-Part Approach 185

   Confrontation When Data is not Available for Spiritual Care 188

   Confrontation About Equity 190

   Other Helpful Ideas, Including Lessons Learned 191

Chapter Fifteen: Prophetic Pastoral Care of Confronting the Truth in Local Churches by Wayne Menking 197

Chapter Sixteen: Confrontation for Certification: Testing Personal and Professional Integration by Gordon J Hilsman 211

   Assessing Integration in Potential Clinical Pastoral Educators 217

   1. Cognitive/Affective Integration 218

   2. Theory/Practice Integration 220

   3. Integration of One's Personal History into Educational Practice Forming a Clinical Educator Identity 221

   4. Therapy/Education Distinction 224

   5. Confrontation for Certification of Chaplains 226

    6. Integration Demonstrated 229

Chapter Seventeen Confronting God: Passionately Addressing the Power Beyond Us All by Gordon J Hilsman 233

    1. Praise or Adoration 234

    2. Gratefulness..235

    3. Regret, Sorrow 236

    4. Petition 236

    5. Protest 237

EPILOGUE ONE Five Confrontations I've Needed in My Lifetime that Never Came by Gordon J Hilsman......................239

    1. Ball Hog 240

    2. Wrong Major 241

    3. Buried Emotions 242

    4. Lagging Integrity 243

    5. Painful Neglect 244

EPILOGUE TWO Skills Not Easily Learned by Sandra Walker 247

DEDICATION

This book is dedicated to the editors' siblings –
Joyce Kemper, June Smith, Patty Summers, and
the Ralston boys: Finnigan, Mike, Phillip, and Donny.
They were our first peer confronters.

FOREWORD:

By
The Rev Karen Hutt
Certified Clinical Educator
Minneapolis MN

Since moving to the Upper Midwest, I have become very fond of Aspen trees. A casual glance at the Northwoods horizon gives the impression that each tree is distinct and independent of one another. Yet, underground, these trees are all connected to one powerful root that keeps creating new and unique approaches to being an Aspen tree. When I contemplate the roots of Clinical Pastoral Education, I consider Gordon Hilsman to be one of those powerful roots that continues to seed propositions and ideas that demand our attention in chaplaincy and clinical pastoral education.

When I first encountered his earlier book, *Intimate Spirituality: The Catholic Way of Love and Sex* [1]. I was working with a group of Dominican Catholic sisters in a Level One CPE unit in Illinois. As a Black Humanist Unitarian Universalist minister, I listened closely as these lay women were navigating the complexity of family systems, sexism, and their varied understanding of what it meant to be an embodied Catholic. One of them brought forward Hilsman's book and said, "This book might move us to think differently, so we might serve the real issues some of these families are dealing with without the priest looking over our shoulder." In a chapter titled *"Sacramental Enhancement: Can*

Agape Learn from Eros?" The Dominican sisters began to create new options by squarely confronting long held tropes, misinformation and hierarchical edicts that were not useful for the real challenges the families in their care were facing. Hilsman's book helped them confront sexuality in a positive affirmational manner that provided new tools. While these confrontations appeared nominal to those outside the Catholic faith, for these women, it was transformational and life-giving.

As a CPE student and educator in training, I was invited to reflect on my growing edges, tender points and shadow selves. This work was painful, necessary and at times manipulative and indirect. The language around these processes always seemed coded in metaphors or attached to theoretical construct boxes. The word that was always missing for me was confrontation.

In my early work as a chaplain, I described my budding practice as one of "presence." I sought to be as gray, as innocuous and middle of the road as possible. I believed that this posture would provide the "pastoral container," "the needed calm" or a "gentle balm" for those in crisis. More often than not, this insipid neutrality led to equally flaccid conversations. I had acquired this behavior from my nice, midwestern, white, colleagues who were my early models and mentors. This was not working. I was not being true to my natural authentic self; a sardonic, upper middle class, east coast black urbanite. The needed act of "soul shaping" that Hilsman describes in *How to Get the Most Out of Clinical Pastoral Education: A CPE Primer* [2] needed to be addressed, so I changed my approach to be more confrontational, more direct and more truly myself.

When the death penalty ended in Illinois, I was charged to provide care for those men transitioning from death row to the general prison population. On the long bus ride with shackles clanging on a prison bus, one of the men yelled to me in a threatening tone, "Yeah chaplain, we have been preparing to die for twenty years, how are you gonna teach us to live?" I knew that I had to respond in a manner that might lead to a working trusting relationship, so without hesitation I yelled back to him, "What is your life worth now?" This direct confrontational tone and response was well received, and a conversation began as we drove through the cornfields. Authenticity and context-based confrontation matters.

Later, as a pediatric oncology chaplain, a dad was pointing vigorously at his ten-year-old son, as he described the aggressive nature of the cancer. In fact, each time he talked about his son he referred to cancer. His son was visibly annoyed and appeared to shrink into the bed every time his father spoke.

> I finally said, "Wait a minute dad, just wait a minute. Who is in that bed?"

> He looked bewildered and said "What do you mean?"'

> I repeated my question and he said, "my son."

> I said, "Your son is not cancer, your son has a name, and you need to use his name, to remind him that you see him."

His son chimed in and said, "Yeah dad, I am not just a bunch of bad cells. I am the same kid you had before I was sick"

This was the risky confrontation that was needed to provide care.

In both these situations, confrontation paved the way for insight and trust. Direct statements illuminated and increased the congruence between the care-seekers behavior and need. The many paths to confrontation can lead to useful recognition and potential changes in people's emotions, thoughts, and actions.

Hilsman has provided practitioners and educators an important book. As he deconstructs the nature of confrontational spiritual care, he has selected a diverse and extraordinarily competent group of clinicians. Each provides practical real-life examples of their care work using confrontation as an intervention strategy. The skills we can gain from this book are innumerable. If you are a seminary professional, chaplain or educator, this book will help you rethink, revise, and reinvigorate your practice.

---

[1] Gordon Hilsman, *Intimate Spirituality: The Catholic Way of Love and Sex*, (New York: Rowan and Littlefield, 2007)

[2] Gordon Hilsman, *How to Get the Most Out of Clinical Pastoral Education: A CPE Primer*, (Philadelphia: Jessica Kingsley Publishers, 2018)

PREFACE

The 2012 BBC TV film *The Best of Men*,[1] illustrates the effectiveness of combining clearly conveyed empathy with solid challenge in confronting individual patients and an entire system, to move evolution along just a bit. As a German neurologist in England during World War II, Dr. Ludwig Guttman arrives at the Stoke Mandeville Hospital in 1943 charged with caring for military airmen with spinal cord injuries suffered while landing planes in combat. He found there, all young men, languishing to death with supportive treatment only, by a well-meaning staff unfamiliar with any other kind of care.

As the true-to-life story unfolds, Guttman's challenging style of treatment and leadership rescued patients from a downward trajectory towards a solitary death, to hopeful activity and good-natured competition. His innovative challenges eventually developed into today's Paralympics Games with paraplegic athletes contending against one another in international games parallel to the worldwide Olympics tradition.

One way to understand that dramatic turn-around is to ponder the difference between grief and self-pity. The airmen had long ceased grieving and sunken into deadly defeatism. They needed astute and creative confrontation to shake them uniquely and individually into a curious blend of surrender and effort, to stop feeling sorry for themselves and do what they could to better their situations.

It was a partner process to Alcoholics Anonymous, beginning about ten years earlier in Manhattan, NY and

Akron, OH. Distinguishing between the "giving up" of self-pity and the surrender that presages finding brand new combinations of relationships to confront you for your own benefit, is one element of recovery from many kinds of stuck-ness in living.

Effort has abandoned you in self-pity, but finding new, elusive vectors for your effort is the stuff of using defeat and new ways to relate to transformation in your life.

This book illustrates how confrontation as a spiritual care intervention can contribute to wholistic care of patients in nearly every hospital specialty. Written by experienced spiritual care practitioners working in collaboration with interdisciplinary treatment teams, it illustrates how "going against" the ways patients are either caring for themselves or avoiding it, sometimes contributes to the overall health of people suffering spiritually with difficult medical conditions. Confrontation as one intervention used by spiritual caregivers of any discipline, also helps gain access to other chronic and acute spiritual binds of patients that may be unrelated to a current hospitalization.

We use here a broad understanding of what "spiritual" means, encompassing all people, or as many as the caregiver can tolerate, accept, respect, honor, and invest in, as fellow and sister human beings. Pragmatically speaking, a person's unique spirituality is made up of *all we do, believe, say, and learn in order to cope with and enjoy what we cannot control.* It is how we have learned to face an unpredictable, evolving world, and meet the inevitable life challenges that accost us. We can help one another with our unique spiritualities, in various ways, though never perfectly. Confrontation is one of those ways.

The authors of this book spend their workdays doing their best to assist the human spirits of people besieged by common illnesses, injuries and chronic conditions that are needing professional medical help and other special forms of care. Some of these professional spiritual clinicians are more involved in assisting caregivers than the medically challenged. But all of them know how human need generally remains veiled under a variety of protective cloaks and overlays of distorted or minimized emotion about something else. In those situations, troubled people need a bridge to new understanding. Confrontation is one of those bridges.

All of these authors are convinced that sometimes going against the current flow of reverie and verbal disclosure emanating from a patient, can introduce greater authenticity and soul clearing depth to a caring conversation. Nobody knows what percentage of the time this is true for patients—research may someday give us a ballpark answer. But for now, this book is intended to encourage spiritual caregivers to use their intuition, interpersonal courage, and genuine care to continue practicing and improving the art of confrontation all through their careers.

The world context in which this book is written is made up of seemingly unprecedented churning of conflicts in many aspects of life, from politics and combat to the internet and families. Some of us see this as a considerable shift in evolutionary movement. Hospitals, always a concentration of problems beyond the adequacy of our own self-care, can be seen as microcosms of that upheaval in which we humans are hounded by decision after decision of what to silently tolerate, support and accept on the one hand, and what to contend with and confront on the other.

Such decisions are the normal mini culture of the hospital milieu. Expressions of empathy and support stand constantly beside needs to "go against" in order to care. These authors intend here to open up the ways in which they fit confrontation into the complex scenarios of the unique spiritual needs of patients and others for whom they care.

Chapter one begins the perspective of intertwining empathy with confrontation, and in chapter two a retired ACPE certified educator recalls the way in which a single confrontation can change a life direction, as it did his.

Well educated chaplains and other spiritual caregivers as subjects here are not merely supportive, accommodating, religio-spiritual encouragers. Some of them are accepting the call to learn new intricate skills to uncover serious underlying personal and interpersonal issues like the potential drinking problems that come closest to being amenable to help when hospitalized (Chapter 3). In Chapter 4 an exceptional palliative care physician describes his central role in ways that fit spiritual caregivers as sometimes key actors in the process of treatment until there is no more treatment, only human care. From dying in hospice, to subsisting on the street, to frantic efforts to keep your child alive in pediatrics, the perspectives loosened by confrontation add or enhances the practice of spiritual care by any discipline interested in augmenting the human spirit when it is accosted by illness, injury, unfortunate conditions, and the dying process.

---

[1] *The Best of Men,* directed by Tim Whitby (BBC, 2012).

DISCLAIMER PLUS

While the editors for this book have been highly active for decades in the primary professional organizations of the clinical ministry movement, none of the opinions and stances in this book represent any of those associations. Nor do these chapter authors necessarily agree with one another on this topic. We, and the other authors of these chapters, speak for ourselves not our organizations or professional associations. The cases and vignettes we offer here are all composites of pieces of information from different events mixed together to protect the confidentiality of all concerned.

    The caption under my high school yearbook picture read simply, "A gentleman knows how to disagree without being disagreeable." It looked good, sounded cool, and even seemed to fit me then. But it didn't turn out to be true. I've often been a regretting coward in the midst of conflict and unpleasantness on the one hand, and nastily unkind with the bare truth as I saw it on the other. But whoever chose that quote for me did me a great service. It stuck in my mind that there is something both honorable and becoming in being able to engage unpleasant issues and events in some potentially helpful way. I've done my best at that, though it hasn't always been good enough. This book is largely what I've learned the hard way from mistakes and from observing other expert confronters engaging conflict and unlocking the deeper currents underneath the surface in troubled people.

My co-editor likewise did not come naturally to valuing confrontation so highly that she would invest in creating a book about it. She writes: "Confrontation did not come easily to me either. Like many young girls, I was conditioned to acquiesce, comply, and conform. I learned to silence my feelings, perspectives, and perceptions in favor of others. It was not until my early thirties that I found my voice. As a young woman crossing the developmental threshold into adulthood, I challenged the myth of an idealized childhood as I confronted my parents with the failures and blessings of their nurturing. A therapeutic reenactment subsequently, appropriately, and painfully played out by my own children years later. That formative confrontation set me on a path to more sustainable, reliable, dependable, and authentic relationships."

This book is mostly for caregivers of any discipline who remain perpetually fascinated with the helping dialogue. That means people who frequently involve themselves with the human spirit of people in difficult times, seeking to briefly join them, hear them and do what they can to respond to their plight at hand. It includes physicians and nurses who appreciate the personal, interpersonal, and existential complications of illness and injury, as well as institutional spiritual caregivers or chaplains who engage the spirits of troubled people as professionals in our own right.

The latter are especially our target audience since we spiritual caregivers tend to be super nice avoiders of conflict, subtly steering clear of angry people and unpleasant situations that might unmask us as incompetent nincompoops. An evolutionary world is necessarily filled with conflicts large and small, and we remain irrelevant until we get that deeply into our makeup. Even then we only begin to learn aspects of the art of confronting those conscious and unconscious habits and conditions that perennially keep troubled humans stuck like the wounded farm dog alone under the porch. Beneficial confrontation comes almost magically from people who care deeply, honor the power of directness of words in key situations, distinguish confrontation clearly from ridicule or cynicism, and listen to their intuition that awakens but doesn't always make logical sense. Such people are genuine gems in a world of mediocre costume jewelry.

Only a few people seem to be constitutionally suited to this interpersonal competency. But all of us can do it well enough. We can grasp and incorporate it as one acquired skill to enrich the quality of our care of people. None of us is born confronting well. But we can always keep on learning.

If you look for perfection, or even excellence in your confronting, you will only find it episodically, like home runs by the best baseball hitters. But when it is done even reasonably well with genuine care for this particular troubled person, honest, astute engagement will feel to them like the scales of Paul of Tarsus falling from their eyes. You will mostly never see that new, transforming recognition in those you confront. But you will often feel it richly within you.

ACKNOWLEDGMENTS

As editors, we salute, first, those who starkly and pointedly confronted us in our families, our grade school classes, on our teams, in seminary and CPE, and in our preparation for careers as certified clinical educators, in ways that touched and hammered us into what we are now. We also thank those expert practitioners who penned the chapters of this book in the midst of their busy careers and their deft dodging of Covid-19. We must include those equally proficient chaplains and educators who promised chapters on such other worthy topics as—facilitating the "coming out" process; managing spiritual care departments amidst their chaplains' entitlement and conflict avoidance; confronting highly disciplined military chaplains a step above you in the chain of command; and several other specialized situations—but were unable to deliver. May your writing find other venues and publications for your success.

I especially include here Stephanie Worley, Mary Jane O'Neil, Bernie Pennington, Joan Armstrong, and Juan Iregui for their unforgettable styles of confronting that amazed me, and to some degree demonstrated to me the beauty of caring confrontation. Especially my wife Nancy, who tried so often to smooth the edges of my bald starkness and almost succeeded. God love her. I sure do. And my three children who did so at various times, too, from my daughter who confronted me at 30 months and again when I was 67, my one son at age 11, and the other at 14. It all has led to the most treasured events of intimacy from which I have benefitted in my development. Thank you all from my deepest core.

Sandy Walker, my co-editor, writes: "I am ever grateful for the clarity, fidelity, and support of my early mentors Ron Evans, Marlo Peterson, Jon De Yong, and Robert Grigsby. And to my companions on this journey, my beloveds, Dale, Ben, Sam and Mandy.

Finally, my friend and colleague, artist/author/publisher and clergyman Joel Graves, who made the technical aspects of this project even possible.

PART ONE:

Empathy's Partner:
The Enigmatic Nature and Value of Confrontation

Chapter One:

The Face-to-Face Gateway in Spiritual Care
by
Gordon J Hilsman

If we had to choose only one spiritual care intervention from among all those listed in published taxonomies, curriculum summaries, certification competency lists, and research articles, it would have to be conveying empathy. To astound a patient with clear indication that another person grasps their primary emotions in that always unique predicament is a goal of most every spiritual care effort. That is because decades of chaplaincy experience have shown it, and, as Harvard psychiatrist Greg Fricchione has documented scientifically, personal isolation is the first deep experience of serious health issues, one that yearns for healing connection by loving care.[1] In short, nobody understands what it is like to be that specific person in that unique life situation. Some level of felt loneliness is almost always involved, whether it shows or not. Genuine empathy conveyed well dispels that loneliness, albeit temporarily, like nothing else.

But as the phenomenon of long-term systemic racism in the United States has shown, *empathy is often not enough.* Personal presence can be powerfully caring, but it can also be an excuse for inexperienced passivity or even fearful petrification. As one young ICU patient's irate mother once said crisply to a neophyte chaplain, "Well, aren't you going to say anything. All I'm seeing is a lot of standing around and shifting from one foot to another!"

Genuine empathy cries out for action, if only to promote more disclosure. There are times when empathy without something else does little more than Charlie Brown telling Snoopy, shivering in the snow, "Be joyful and well fed," and walking away. A piece of that action called for after conveying empathy is sometimes the depth of quiet presence. But sometimes it is the face-to-face courageous truth of confrontation.

Ralph L Underwood offers a concise way of understanding the partnership between empathy and confrontation. As a Christian theologian, Underwood writes with the traditional language of that perspective, yet captures the human relationship succinctly:

> "In empathic listening, the pastor's own viewpoint is held in check to ensure accurate and caring understanding of the other person. In confrontation a perspective other than the parishioner's own is introduced…Even when understanding is advanced through empathy, the stimulation of an additional approach may be immensely useful. On the other hand, confrontation that presumes to proceed without empathy often misses the mark as well as provoking unnecessary opposition and defensiveness." [2]

A mild and kind form of confrontation promotes further disclosure by most patients. In the early development of the clinical ministry movement, one of the several ingredients besides Freudian psychoanalysis, Jungian depth psychology, and fledgling group therapy, was the existentialists' phenomenology, inspired by the German Jewish philosopher Edmund Husserl. Briefly he taught that we can never see the noumenon, what actually exists; but only the phenomenon, the thing as it appears to us. Existentialist therapists took that to refer to how, if you describe a person as you apprehend them at any given moment, you stimulate them to further disclose themselves. A classic learning of CPE students is how to describe one another accurately as we see one another, to foster relationship. The ability to fashion those varying mini-descriptions adds up to some of the most valuable feedback students learn in their entire lifetimes and prepares them to represent patient spiritual needs usefully in the medical record.

Gaining access to the inner world of people for their own benefit has long been a basic function of spiritual caregiving. Chaplains and pastoral counselors facilitate sharing from the depths of a person, from the patient's own point of view. The traditional disciplines of medicine and nursing, for which hospitals were designed, have a primary need of *diagnostic* listening. Chaplains, who on the other hand are skilled at *personal* listening. Since the beginning of the clinical ministry movement in the mid-1920s, spiritual care (then, and sometimes now, known as pastoral care) has been incorporating the perspectives of other caregiving disciplines into its practice.

That newer clinical style of spiritual care, as notably described succinctly by Howard Clinebell, uses four types of interventions: *empathy, questions, interpretations, and support* to establish rapport, and then uses that initial relationship to facilitate further disclosures and emotions.[3] That basic framework has been a top tool in evaluating pastoral care conversations of clinical pastoral education (CPE) students ever since. Clinebell did not champion confrontation centrally in that book. He did, however, mention it briefly there and addresses it effectively in his books on care of alcoholics. And confrontation now needs to be seen far more broadly.

The confrontation intervention can be seen as either an addition to Clinebell's four types as a distinct fifth element, or preferably, as in a class of its own that can take the form of any of the others, except support. Better yet, it can be seen as the partner of conveyed empathy, used as either a *question*, a *reflective comment*, or an *interpretation*, that invites a person to another level of depth of disclosure and conversation. Here are three personal examples of confrontations in the form of an astute emotional *reflection*, a sharp intuitive *interpretation*, and a savvy, pointed *question*.

Confrontation as Emotional Reflection

In my third unit of CPE, I was once talking in group ever more openly than I had anticipated. At one point a peer simply said gently, "It sounds like you've been lonely most of your life." As a celibate priest at 31 years old, I was hit by that like the proverbial ton of bricks. I'd never seen myself as lonely but rather successful, compelling, inward, and inhibited. I had however, chronically recognized a vague, unnamed feeling of awkward sadness as quite familiar. My peer was calling it correctly. It was so true and clear, so pointed and insightful, it made me shiver and I could not ignore it. I didn't cry then, sitting in my stunned silence, but I did profusely later that day.

<blockquote align="center">That was a confrontation in the shape
of an empathic reflection.</blockquote>

Confrontation as an Interpretation

After that third CPE unit, I met a committee for consultation requesting what was then called "advanced standing" in the ACPE. In the consultation group of six, as I followed the lines of inquiry and responded as openly as I could, one consultant leaned forward, looked me in the eye with a smile, and said, "Sounds like what you really want is to be celibate one day a week, married one day a week, and single five days a week!". Everyone laughed but me. That was one of those "funny, but not funny" comments that invites one into a different perspective entirely, exactly what confrontation always attempts to do.

It was confrontation as an *interpretation,* an adding of insight to a situation that will hopefully crack it open. That one did, for me.

Confrontation as a Question

Later, after final educator certification, I was still stuck in ambivalence for months over leaving the priesthood. I was involved with a woman but functioning publicly as a celibate, putting off the most painful decision of my life. As I shared my situation openly with a brilliant friend and author two years younger than me, he asked, "Can't you find a way to be both sexual and celibate?" Wham. My reflexive response betrayed the deeper truth. "Dan, I've got to get some integrity back into my life." No! blared clearly now in my mind. That question suggested something loathsome to me. I knew priests who had fathered children and were still functioning as priests. I simply couldn't even consider it. It was immediately clear that I had only one direction that would get me whole. I followed through with the process of laicization soon after.

That was a confrontation in the form of a simple *question.*

We humans are not open books. Sometimes we need help turning that front cover over to see our own pages and begin perusing deep inside.

Humans are rarely direct in dealing with our serious needs. We do *display* some of our serious concerns to all the world, especially when we feel like we must do so for a little longer survival, or for a manipulative edge in tight situations. We sometimes *intentionally hide* what bothers us most for the sake of managing our image or protecting people we love from the truth. But most often we curiously have many concerns *hidden from ourselves* by variously named unconscious processes of which we are not in charge. Self-deceit still abounds at this stage of the evolution of humanity

Like the world's rivers to our human ancestors, there are natural barriers to our moving freely into personal openness; and like the fences we ourselves build for protection, there are unique ways we shield ourselves from feeling the stark truths of our difficulties too vividly. We keep some distance from our own souls…until we don't.

At times we need bridges over our natural river barriers and gateways through our self-constructed fences into our own radical self-awareness. Spiritual caregivers sometimes need to use those gateways to really hear troubled peoples' pains and respond creatively to them. Prime among those gateways is the remarkable skill of confrontation in its innumerable forms.

Of course, not all confrontive interventions are dramatic or obviously transformational.

Consider, for example, this male patient experiencing prior grief, the common, even universal awakening of feelings of sadness, regret, warmth, and malaise relative to remembering a major loss long after it happened. The vague feelings of major loss lay there, maybe unpredictably felt often, and are brought near the surface of consciousness by the experience of hospitalization. A chaplain visits this man for the first time.

In a common spiritual care conversation in a hospital room, the male patient is talking briefly about himself.

> He mentions, "…then, just after my wife died…." He finishes the sentence and moves on. A moment later, he pauses.

The chaplain simply asks, "Wait. Did you say your wife died?"

Patient: "Yeah. She passed away right here in this hospital." After a second, he adds, "My son lives just over in Fremont."

Chaplain, quietly, "How did she die?"

Patient: "Oh, she got cancer and was gone in three months." Again, he pauses. "My sister died last year too, up in Montana".

The chaplain waits a moment then says, "Your wife died quickly—I'm sorry—she was pretty young."

Patient: "Yeah. We thought we'd have a lot more time."

The chaplain says slowly, patiently, "Sad. Disappointing. Think about her a lot?"

Patient: "Oh God yeah. All the time. Every day. We had our differences, but she was a wonderful woman."

Chaplain: "Lots of memories flood you I bet, sometimes."

The patient looks out the window and becomes teary. "I cry sometimes when I remember.

Cry hard sometimes. I remember...." He goes on reminiscing.

At least twice here, the chaplain confronts the patient in a gently empathic, but quietly firm way. Both times she "goes against" the prevailing thinking process in the man and draws his attention to his wife and the grief the chaplain believes lies in wait, ready to be shared, again, in the process of the man's underlying grieving experience. The conversation may have brought the man to his covert grief without the mild confrontation, but probably not. It is possible, too, that there was something else the man needed to talk about that was missed by the chaplain turning the conversation to the prior grief. But not much could have been more important. Reminiscing about his wife, which now may take 15 or 20 minutes, probably contributes positively to his spirit this day and his potential ability to cope and heal in this hospitalization.

There may be controversy about whether reminiscing can be harmful to some people with trauma histories, and thus not advisable in the short window of time with which chaplains work. But such highly sensitized patients are generally recognizable by facial vulnerability, shaky demeanor, and pace of speaking. We can assume that the experienced chaplain proceeds to explore the grieving after quickly making that appraisal—this soul is ready to reminisce.

Even very experienced caregivers may not have interrupted the man's flow of disclosure. That said, confrontation most always includes the possibility of failure. Courage to proceed judiciously with the willingness to apologize gracefully, if necessary, is a skill to be developed by all chaplains.

Hospitalized people fairly-often regress. When placed in that vulnerable personal place many of us take refuge in ways of coping we don't normally use, becoming more like children, even toddlers. Adults crying, bickering, opposing, demanding, and insulting are fairly common in hospitals. In that vein spiritual care is sometimes more like parenting a toddler than an infant. Rather than needing total support and warmth, like an infant, conflict is natural for a toddler. Two-year-old children demand it, insist on it, force it. They will not survive without it. Mild or sharp confrontation, in rare cases even physical restraint forms an integral part of their care. And their development. Some patients in particular situations are like that. Consciously or unconsciously, they will not feel the care deeply, or find themselves anew, without a strong, observant voice gently finding them.

In an age of a new and hopefully vigorous dealing with systemic racism and a growing awareness of the personal and interpersonal wounding of most women and children in their childhood or youth, we caregivers need our confrontation to be done well, with practice, and continuous, courageous trial and error to constantly get better at it.

Confrontation in spiritual caregiving is leaning into an issue, injecting a tone of intimate connection into a conversation. The moment of confrontation dispenses with congenial social perspectives, formalities, and polite niceties. Confrontation includes the intention to change the way two are meeting to a way that is more direct, engaging and potentially unpleasant, to address important and difficult matters. It is used occasionally by some medical and nursing staff in most every hospital unit and can be employed effectively by chaplains to deepen conversations to a soul-to-soul level while not overwhelming a person with the unavoidable dire tragedy of a situation.

Historically clergy carry that reputation. A special kind of conversation that, in certain circumstances reaches deeper into issues, has always characterized pastoral connection, even before the initiation of the clinical ministry movement began in 1920s America. When one person "levels" with another about serious personal matters in heart-to-heart disclosures and deliberations, souls are reached, relationships altered, and lives are changed. Such interactions often follow the lead of a caregiver who creates an atmosphere for open sharing and authenticity, and then uses it to bring the most difficult disclosures of the patient to the surface. That caregiver shows in the dialogue, by manner and tone, that they have the time, the interest, the earthiness, and the interpersonal courage to stand face-to-face, willing to be honest in delicate, discouraging, or personally scary matters. That is confrontation in the best sense of the word.

Some spiritual care confrontations are deftly gentle, calmly patient, and carefully direct. Some are much more difficult. For patients who are semi-publicly making racist statements; or showing indication of having a drinking or mental illness problem; or parents clueless about the dire seriousness of their child's medical situation; or combat veterans at a point of ambivalence about sharing the worst of their war experience; caring confrontation may need skillful expertise necessary to further the care, sometimes towards intricate referral to other forms of care.

The primary purpose of this book is to illustrate how confrontation can be used in various aspects of health care and its wider culture, and to promote continually learning to confront as a basic tool for the practice of all caregivers.

The phenomenon of caring confrontation isn't precisely definable in any clearly useful way. We can describe it however, as *one person bringing clearly to another, an observed or intuited truth that may be unpleasant but is likely to reduce that person's self-deception and improve the quality of their self-awareness for care of themselves and other people.* The authors will be demonstrating how this can be done effectively and more often in difficult spiritual care conversations.

Piercing the Music: Finding Your Soul to Midwife 'the New' in Interpersonal Care

Usually, one needs to find one's own soul to confront well. It takes reflection, allowing the situation to affect you, tuning into your intuitive grasp of the situation as a whole, employing your own personal or caregiving history of similar difficulties, and then finding words and phrases to boldly, succinctly yet kindly and humanly, convey your unique take on it. This seems like a daunting task. It can be. And then again, at times it merely leaps to your mind as a sincere caregiver moved by jarring empathy. Call it the Spirit of God or the mysterious genius of the human personality. Either way it commands the situation and cares for this person, now, on a level that is impossible without addressing the issue directly.

The ordinary, mostly social lubricative interaction that provides pleasant, congenial connections between people in everyday life is musical. It makes life warmer, more pleasant, more connected, and more fun. In small process groups however, and in spiritual care of people in difficult life situations, social comments are often less useful. They can become like music turned into noise, distracting and even annoying. There are times when personally light and supportive efforts at comfort, run the course of their usefulness. Then instead, they obstruct interaction that could be more beneficial to all of those involved.

As philosopher/humorist Stendhal wrote in the nineteenth century:

> *"Oh, if only there were a true religion. Fool that I am, I see a Gothic cathedral and venerable stained-glass windows, and my weak heart conjures up the priest to fit the scene. My soul would understand him, my soul has need of him. I only find a nincompoop with dirty hair."* [4]

Those times call for a confrontation versus continued superficializing collusion—a statement by one person who sees the relevant deep truth of a situation and finds a sharp but relatively palatable way of expressing it in clear words.

This is deep and soulful human encounter. Soul here means the core of a person, the unique inner depth that motivates humans non-verbally and can be partially seen by observing the spirit, the elan, the excitement or discouragement of the person. Soul is the seat of a person's values and one's pursuit of them. What is called spiritual or pastoral care is a soul-to-soul interaction that transcends the social and especially the pedantic instructional.

Beware. Understanding and appreciating confrontation belies the fact that confronting is most often interpersonally dangerous. It always carries the likelihood that it will tweak the ire of any or all of those involved, and even, in some cases, interloping bystanders. When one person notices and verbalizes a deeper truth, those around can easily misunderstand. But those who are open and savvy, will see the new perspective and be grateful for it.

When Not to Confront
(or to not confront again)

Here are examples of some situations in which it may be better for a spiritual caregiver to back off and deftly attempt referral to another form of care.

• Before you have developed at least minimal skills of conveying empathy.

• When at least a minimal level of rapport has not yet been established.

• When dealing with persons with a known history of unintegrated trauma.

• When a person is psychotically or characteriologically violent.

Figure 1

Contact Info: Gordon Hilsman   ghilsman@gmail.com

and www.SpiritualClinician.com

[1] Gregory Fricchione, *Compassion and Healing in Medicine and Society: The Nature and Use of Attachment Solutions to Separation Challenges,* (Baltimore: Johns Hopkins University Press, 2011).

[2] Ralph L. Underwood, *Empathy and Confrontation in Pastoral Care* (Eugene: Wipf and Stock Publishers, 2002), 89. Note: Previously published by Augsburg Fortress Publishers, 1985.

[3] Howard Clinebell, *Basic Types of Pastoral Care and Counseling Revised: Resources for the Ministry of Healing and Growth* (Nashville: Abingdon Press, 2011), 21-43

[4] Henri Beyle Stendhal, *The Red and the Black: A Chronicle of 1830* (Public Domain)

Chapter Two:

The Transforming Potential of Being Confronted by Wes McIntyre

Despite the clear contract CPE students make in entering a program, to give and receive direct feedback on our caregiving relationships, due to the hiding, confusing, and abrasive aspects of our personalities, there is still considerable resistance to learning in clinical education. Resistance in this educational context refers to the unique set of habits, patterns and attitudes that hold back our careful and authentic looking at ourselves and our caring relationships in order to improve them. Supervising that learning process thus requires considerable confrontation in the personal shaping required for becoming a clinical pastoral educator. It takes four to five years of practice under observation and after a master's degree and a residency for certification as a chaplain. Changes need to take place inside us that don't come easily. Simply describing accurately what they see, clinical supervisors often jolt budding educators with what some have come to call "truth bombs." Retired educator Wes illustrates that here.

I arrived for the beginning of my CPE residency after completing my M.Div., becoming ordained, pastoring a small rural church for nine years, and struggling through a year's leave of absence from any pastoral appointments. I was depressed and desperate to find a way both to follow my call and support my family. In the fourth week of my first unit of training, my CPE supervisor closed our individual supervisory appointment with these words, "Wes, one thing for certain is that you are going to have to decide what to do with your arrogance."

I don't recall making any response to him at the time. But inside of me I began a serious interrogation about the meaning of arrogance in relation to how I saw and understood myself. No-one had ever called me arrogant before. I hadn't ever thought of myself as arrogant. His statement stopped my world.

I was committed to not waste the opportunities CPE provided. I had already decided to always reflect on statements made by asking myself, "If it were true, how would that look, how could that be so?" But in the days that followed I could not make a connection between myself and my supervisor's assessment of me. Still, I kept hearing his voice in my head, "....you are going to have to decide what to do with your arrogance."

Then, one afternoon, I was visiting Ellie, an 84-year-old woman and patient on the cardiac unit I was assigned to. We got introduced, I sat near her bed, and we began to talk. Helen voiced a question that carried a mind tone of lament. "Why do you think they call these the golden years?" Before I could respond, she went on, "Anymore my eyes are so bad I can't read." Her lament was building up some steam, "I can't hardly taste my food anymore. And I can't hear you chaplain. You have got to speak up. And I can't even decide when to pee anymore!" After a pause her voice changed and she asked, "Why is it that God made it that way?"

My mind raced, searching for the answer and I heard my supervisor's words again, "Wes…..you are going to have to decide what to do with your arrogance." In that moment I got it! That is when the 40-year-old chaplain intern turned to the 84-year-old woman in her bed, and said, "Ellie, you have obviously thought way more about that question than I have. What do you think is the answer?" Ellie looked me in the eye and stated matter-of-factly, "I don't think there is an answer." I paused, in new territory here, having let go of the role as the answer man, and then said, "Well Ellie, what do you do with that?" Her head dropped and she seemed to look inward for a moment, and when her head came up, her face lit with a different countenance, and she said, "I just hang onto the love of God."

That was not the end of the visit nor was it the end of my learning from my supervisor's confrontation. In the next individualized supervisory conference, I told him about this visit with Ellie and what happened for Ellie and for me in those moments. We talked together about arrogance and he finished that session saying, "Arrogance isn't such a bad thing. You have to be a little arrogant to think you can teach anything to anyone." I still hear that veteran educator's voice to this day.   The second experience of confrontation I want to mention occurred in CPE class during our group interpersonal relations time. I had initiated a conversation with a peer regarding her negligence in passing on the on-call pager at the agreed upon times. After some time, the supervisor for this session said to the group, "Aren't you all just getting tired of this? I am!" I was startled. And the supervisor saw it on my face. After a pause, during which no one in the group spoke out, he turned to me and said in his Southern drawl, "Well Wes, you just keep sounding like such a victim." This too was an assessment I had not encountered before, and I was at a loss to know how or why it could be true. And again. it sent me into a reflective process, pursuing information about victimhood, recognizing my own behaviors that matched that role and discovering the alternatives for engaging myself and others in new and more productive ways.

The third and last confrontation I want to present here took place in a certification committee meeting during my training process to become certified as an ACPE Certified Educator. I was a little over half-way through my supervisory training and was seeking an extension of my training status with a regional certification committee. After addressing the committee for about ten minutes regarding why I was there and responding to the presenter's report, one committee member said to me, "I have been sitting here trying to imagine what it is like to supervise students the way you do and I am about to puke." I was startled by the statement; confused by what in my presentation made him ill, and at a loss to know how to respond to what seemed like a bullying or intimidating statement. No other committee member spoke and to this day I don't recall what about my presentation prompted his statement.

The first two conversations had the following elements. There was an ongoing relationship with the confronter, I had a level of trust in the confronters that assumed they had my best interest in mind, each confrontation carried a descriptive observation or assessment about my person and/or behavior, and both were available in an ongoing fashion to continue the conversation.

The third confrontation did not contain an ongoing relationship or learning contract, it lacked any assessment or observation of me that was discernable, the motive for it was undiscernible to me though it seemed like some display of dominance and thus in the interest of the confronter rather than in the interest of my learning or growth, and there was no ongoing conversation offered or desired by me.

Perhaps before confrontations are utilized it would be good to ask oneself the following questions:

1. What observation or assessment of this person am I clear about that they need to hear?

- As a test for my own clarity, can I objectively describe behavior that informs my assessment or illustrates my observation?

- Have I observed this behavior, characteristic, trait, event more than once; is it a pattern?

- Are there others who have also witnessed this, and do I think they would agree with my observation or assessment?

2. What level of relationship do I have with this person and/or is needed in order to connect with this person in an effective way?

- What is the history of my relationship with this person?

- Are we new to each other or well acquainted?

- Is this relationship contractual, formal, informal, other?

- Do we have a "track record" with each other that would indicate that confrontation is expected, desired, and/or welcomed?

- What is the power differential between us and how can that be best used to make this confrontation effective, as in service to the one being confronted?

3. How might I engender enough trust to be taken both seriously and genuinely caring if I become clear with this person about his/herself as I am seeing them? Things to consider include:

- The context of the confrontation and its probable impact on the person's receptivity and thus, the ability to focus on what is offered.

- How does this person expect or prefer to be addressed?

- What emotional energy do I have about this potential confrontation, and will it be useful or not in this conversation or relationship?

- Do I communicate a demand by my tone of voice; arrogance; or is my voice invitational?

- Am I making the confrontation as the end of the matter or am I eliciting a response that can then be responded to for clarification and more engagement?

- Do I care enough about this person to extend an invitation to process this further?

4. Do I care enough about this person to extend an invitation to process this further?

- Am I making the confrontation as the end of the matter or am I eliciting a response that can then be responded to for clarification and more engagement?

- And also, if the person confronted seems mystified, or confused by the confrontation, would you offer them a chance to consider it and come back to talk more about it later?

Being seriously confronted about one's core being is very often memorable and life changing. It deserves careful thought and preparation.

Contact Info: Wes McIntyre, Pasco WA
pascopadre@gmail.com

PART TWO:

Faces of Confrontive Patient Care

Chapter Three:

The Unconsciously Hidden: Potential Drinking Problems in the General Hospital
by
Gordon J Hilsman

A nasty truth we like to ignore or even hide, is that chaplains mostly pass by the rooms of patients who may be afflicted with the illness that is the cause of more family pain than anything else, alcoholism. Alcoholics Anonymous was created by miserable drunks desperately seeking a way to stop drinking alcohol in the mid-1930s. Their forbears having gotten little or no help in past millennia from medicine, religion, government, and law, they stumbled upon some new understanding they fashioned into Twelve Steps by which they were staying sober through a unique quality interaction with one another. The following is a description of a few skills that spiritual caregivers can learn to reduce chaplain helplessness in this area, to engage situations in which there is reason to believe there may be a drinking problem, and even alcoholism, afoot. They include a soft and tough approach, remaining personally confident with realistic expectations of outcomes. As a chaplain develops these skills, they will be helping problem drinkers even though the positive outcomes will almost never be seen.

After three units of clinical pastoral education, I was home in the church rectory in Rockwell, Iowa when a CPE supervisor (now clinical educator) called to offer me a supervisory residency at Presbyterian St. Luke's Medical Center in Chicago. The next part of the conversation went like this.

>Me: "Where in the hospital is it? What specialty?"

>Bernie: "It's in a new alcoholism treatment program in Psychiatry."

>Me: "Oh Gees. I don't want that!"

>Bernie: "Why not?"

>Me: "I want to be a general hospital chaplain. I don't want to get that specialized."

>Bernie: "That only shows how little you know about alcoholism. It's in every unit of your hospital. That illness causes all kinds of medical problems that get people hospitalized. You'll never regret learning something real about it."

I took the residency and indeed have never regretted getting immersed in it. What is still true is that most chaplains avoid any serious engagement of patients who may have a drinking problem. We could read and even write tomes about the illness without getting much practical skill in caring for it. But there are such skills. And they can be described briefly in this chapter. Described but not incorporated into a practice. That will take repetitive effort, frequent feelings of failure, and being able to endure quite a lot of misunderstanding along the way. Especially in the encounters that involve a deft, persistent line of gentle but courageous confrontation—a chaplain's best chance of providing real help.

There is no such thing as a typical alcoholic. That idea that there is, frustrates most real help for people who suffer alone with a drinking problem. Such people are legion, and most of them probably look a lot like you. Research shows that they comprise somewhere between 10 and 35 percent of hospital patients. It also shows that if a physician doesn't mention drinking as a problem, patients aren't likely to listen much to anybody else about it. And those with the illness of alcoholism (as distinct from many problems that arise from drinking too much alcohol) will need to hear it many times before the realization occurs. So be prepared to be spurned repeatedly if you invest in caring for them.

Also, learn to completely rid yourself of moralism before you embark on this care. They will smell it in the air almost before they see you. They likely became accustomed to any form of moralism decades ago, if they are old enough. As a chaplain however, you likely have two things going for you in engaging them.

The first is that you have developed a very broad concept of spirituality from which you care for peoples' spirits. The Twelve Step recovery process can be characterized as a deeply spiritual one—if you don't insist on being religious. Religion, in general, and God in particular, evoke in seasoned drinkers mostly feelings of sadness, guilt, fear, inadequacy, and deep hurt. None of those are very effective in promoting recovery. Many alcoholics, as a subset of people with drinking problems, reflexively defend themselves strongly against both religious and spiritual language. But even a few minutes of calm conversation with a healthily religious figure can be valuable to the life of these quietly suffering individuals.

Secondly, there is a window of vulnerability when a problem drinker is hospitalized. It's not wide or lasting, but it does provide an opportunity for them to be serious and speak courageously about their own life. An open, accepting, calm, and savvy looking face may just get through the fog in which they are likely to be living. But it takes a unique set of skills and attitudes to midwife them into getting the help they both desperately need and impulsively avoid.

So, what are the skills?

(Dialogue here represents the patient as a male, though now about 45% of alcoholics are women. All of the original AA members were probably male).

1. First, prepare yourself.

This conversation will likely not be easy. Remind yourself that this person you are about to converse with is one fine individual and will appreciate your slightly formal, open, serious manner, whatever transpires. If this person may have a drinking problem, be prepared to follow the conversation closely and say what you want to say without social banter or attempts at humor. The patient may be in a quite pensive mood, and that will be to your advantage. If the person is an experienced alcoholic, they will be trying to defeat you and at the same time, deep down, hope you "win."

2. Remind yourself of your agenda.

The term "agenda" has a bad rap in early clinical spiritual education. What a neophyte student is needing to do first is to recognize their own goals for the conversation that have been hidden from themselves—their hidden agenda. As experience shapes chaplains, it makes much more sense to stop inventing the wheel with every patient when there are observable patterns that are common. At the same time, be suspicious of your own patterns. Repetition quickly steals your authenticity.

Potential drinking problems are an agenda example. While there may be several issues to address in a heavy drinker, there is a general tack that can be taken that is likely to serve people who have problems probably caused by drinking.

Briefly, it is to:

a. Have a calm conversation about their own concerns about their drinking.

b. Keep focusing on *their* concerns, deftly, persistently.

c. Take advantage of the mention of the key word—alcoholic. It is never your job to diagnose or even assess a person for alcoholism. But use of the word provides an opportunity to offer some solid, simple and clear instruction on this illness that is still so widely misunderstood.

   d. Your overall aim is to see the patient accept an assessment by a qualified addiction counselor. Have one in your mind, and a phone number.

The following is a description of an effort to peek beneath the massive denial of some people's alcoholism. They are a subset of drinking problems. Don't rule out the possibility that they are alcoholics too soon.

3. Recognition: Clarify the indicator.

Whatever there was that got you thinking that there might be a drinking problem in this person, that is the indicator. And it is *only* an indicator, not a diagnostic certainty or even a solid impression. Resist, at all costs, the temptation to see more than an indicator there. You do need one indicator of a drinking problem. You cannot confront without that. Without identifying what suggested a drinking problem in this person, you literally don't know what you are talking about. You will be no match for the kind of self-deceptive interaction this person may have spent years developing in the service of maintaining a shred of self-esteem amidst horrible events attacking it.

Was the indicator a comment from the patient's spouse, partner, or friend, voicing their frustration about essentially, trying to love this patient? Was it a staff member who shared a comment or charted, or something verbalized by a treatment team member? Was it a wondering by a savvy physician or nurse based on common presenting problems in a hospital setting, such as pneumonia, liver disease, pancreatitis, or failure to thrive (FTT)? Was it a series of comments by the patient suggesting a preoccupation with alcohol, such as requesting you get them a beer? Get it clear in your mind, especially if there have been several such indicators. You may need them in the conversation, though one clear one is enough.

4. Raise the issue.

Shortly after introductory comments, mention the issue of drinking. If you don't and proceed too far down the congenial charade of superficial social chatting, it will become crystal clear to this person why you are *really* visiting them—to get them to do whatever you want them to do. Then their well-established manipulator will have bested yours, sealing off the window of vulnerability that hospitalization creates for finding the narrow path towards real help.

How to raise the issue? That depends on the indicator.

For example, a few days after a vehicle crash, (definitely not while the patient is still drunk), the chaplain greets the patient.

> Chaplain: "I noticed that the ER report says you were apparently drinking before this accident."

Patient: Oh, shit! I had a drink or two at the party. What's wrong with that? And who the hell are you?"

C: "Well, I'm a chaplain here and I'm wondering if you ever have concerns about your drinking?"

P: "What do you mean?"

C. "Just, do you sometimes feel a little negative about some of your drinking?"

P: "I like to drink. It makes me feel good."

C: "I'm sure you feel good most of the time when you drink. But are there times when you wonder, or regret some things?"

P: "Well, I ain't no angel you know."

C: "What kinda stuff are you thinking about?"

P: "Well shit. My wife gets scared when she drives with me sometimes. I ain't proud of that. Hate it when she cries."

C.: "Yeah. Feels bad when she feels scared and cries. Her hurt kind of gets to you."

(silence)

P: "Well, she knew I drank when she married me!"

C: "I suppose. But now she cries when she drives with you, are you're drinking?"

P: "Sometimes."

C: "What does she say to you about your drinking?"

P: "She don't like it. But what ya gonna do?"

C: "Puts you in kind of a bind, huh? She's concerned about your drinking and so are you sometimes too."

P: "Yeah. But I don't like everything she does either."

C: "Right. But you do love each other. Does she say why she gets scared and cries?"

P: "Not really. But I 'spose she doesn't want us to get hurt, or…die."

C: "How long has this been going on, you driving while drinking, she crying scared, and you not liking it either?"

P: "Oh, maybe a year or so."

C: "That must be getting old for her."

The patient is getting a little AA Step One counseling in which, in the window of vulnerability of hospitalization, he is getting close to his feelings of regret that occasionally surface in his daily reverie. Continuing in this vein later in a counseling or AA group/sponsor situation, will expand that awareness until he lets the flood of emotions about the consequences of his drinking settle in his soul. He is a long way from that here. The goal for a chaplain is always to see a patient agree to an assessment by a counselor. That rarely happens. But when it does, that patient will remember that chaplain for a very long time.

The immediate tack of the chaplain is to continue a calm conversation with the patient until there the patient tears up or their anger insists you leave the room. That takes patience. The persistent, calm, soft confrontation can be difficult for the patient to resist. It may be only one percent of what will be required to break through to the ability to give an AA "testimony" of how bad things got, what happened to change that, and how is it now. But it may be the *first* one percent.

The substance of Step One to recovery is a thorough sharing of that load of horrible feelings of guilt, shame, defiance, and utter failure resultant from hiding it all since adolescence. If it is shared enough, all that mass of emotion will return when a situation begins to compel the patient to drink again. The chaplain can facilitate a beginning of that recovery process, though they will likely never get to know it.

5. Focus persistently on the patient's own concerns about their drinking.

That is the primary point of this chapter. In a very real sense, there are two people in that patient: one that maintains a solid "I'm OK" external impression, and another that is inwardly alarmed with concerns about the consequences of their drinking. Your job is to ignore the first and address the second. On some hidden level, that patient has had concerns about their drinking behavior for a long time. But nobody has questioned that impression in any optimally uncomfortable way in that window of vulnerability. This chaplain is now doing that. Keep pressing ahead. And do your best to stay connected personally.

6. Respond to the term "alcoholic" when it is used or use it yourself eventually if the patient doesn't.

The charged word "alcoholic" offers an opportunity to do a bit of education about addiction. The patient will frequently use the term to assert that they are not as bad as somebody else, as in, "You wanna see some drinking, my cousin he does some real drinking. He's an alcoholic."

    C: "Mr. P, how much do you know about alcoholism?"

    P: "I know some people who drink a whole lot and can't stop when they ought to. Alcohol ruins their life."

C: "Well, alcohol does affect some people differently than other people. It is actually an illness. About one in ten people have it. Nobody knows for sure why some people get it and some don't. It shows up as being able to drink more than other people, changes their attitudes, behavior, and memory—gets them into trouble. It's not really how much you drink but how it affects you. You may notice that you can drink more than other people, you sometimes can't remember what happened the night before, and tend to get in trouble when you drink. You tend not to stop drinking when other people do and sneak a drinks alone sometimes. And you may get bothered by some things that happen when you drink."

P: "Yeah?"

C: "Yeah. It eventually causes you trouble in some major area of your life. You ever (been fired from a job? Been in jail? Been told you did stuff the night before that you don't remember?)"

The pace of your questions matters. If it's too fast there is no power in the confrontations. A calm, even leisurely attitude lends seriousness to the questions. The patient may be very familiar with fast talkers as wanting to manipulate them. You don't want to resemble those people. If the patient shows any feeling in their voice or face, consider reflecting it, as a way to promote more specifics of disclosure. But more importantly, to further evoke emotion. Logic is only a small part of the conversation. It is the massive hurt hidden in that mind and body that needs to come to awareness, at its own pace.

And remember, there is little truth in generalities. Specifics evoke feelings, the key to beginning the First Step phase of recovery.

7. Fashion a referral.

Making a referral is an art all its own. Only facilitate a referral after you have seen some significant feelings about the patient's drinking behavior. If you've noticed sadness for example, consider reflecting it, simply as in, "You look a little sad all of a sudden." In the rare hospitalization vulnerability, they may amplify feelings and let loose considerable disclosures they never have talked about before. Keep calm. Success in this kind of key conversation is like the proverbial pigeon in the park. If you chase it, it will flit away. If you sit quietly, it just may come and sit beside you. Don't be surprised if the patient cries. Nor if they stop the session and ask you to leave. Remember, this approach only works rarely all the way to the patient accepting an assessment by a counselor. But it is often burned into the patient's memory in a way you will never know about and become a significant point in the difficult and complex process of early recovery.

At some point, if this process seems to be progressing, you may ask,

>C: "Mr. P, how does it feel talking like this?"

>P: "Kinda good actually."

C: "I know a guy (lady, person, fellow) who talks to people about this stuff every day, for a job. Would you be willing to talk with Terry? I could get them to come over tomorrow, I think."

Part of your preparation is to have a name and a number of somebody who assesses addictions, or in this case, preferably alcoholism, professionally. If the patient asks if you think he is an alcoholic, it may be best to not answer directly. It is somebody else's job to diagnose and treat. It is yours to tease out the concerns at a time and in a way that the patient's emotions may be connected to their words.

8. One step at a time.

Do not get ahead of yourself. It is so easy to launch into excessive teaching, too long, too soon, or too enthusiastically. It is called intellectualizing. It is quickly banned and suppressed in patients in AA meetings and in AA based counseling. Squelch the noise in your communication too. Focus on just the words you want to say. Doff any buddy talk; attempts to join the person. You're not what he needs to recover. But you can be crucial in helping him find what he does need. Picture him sitting in a small group of similarly defeated people being listened to in a brand-new way. You are helping them to take the first or next steps to find that group, in AA or addiction treatment. Also, don't generalize to "addictions" from alcohol. It likely only feeds the intellectualization. It may be seen as somehow cooler to talk about addictions, drugs, cocaine, etc., but alcoholism still causes more family pain than anything else.

And finally, remember, bringing any general hospital patient to assessment of a drinking problem rarely works. Or rather, it may take several times to work. If you had a few minutes of calm conversation about a person's drinking, you have given them a gift: a taste of Step One, the narrow path to recovery. Most people with alcoholism still die from it. If you help a few in your career, allow yourself to feel some satisfaction.

And besides, if you don't go into that room, nobody will get any help at all. Who is there who will talk with him like that? Who can? Even social workers tell me they simply ask people like him if they want to do anything with their drinking problem, accept the answer, note it in the chart, and go on with their day. Even the alcoholic nurses and physicians in recovery (and there are plenty of them on your hospital staff) don't have the time, the skill and the inclination to do so. That's why treatment facilities were created. Help him get there. You'll at least get an education.

Chapter Four:

Confronting Patients and Physician Colleagues in Palliative Care
by
Juan Iregui and Gordon J. Hilsman

In the 2011 Joe Carnahan film, The Grey,[1] wolf hunter John Ottway (Liam Neeson) is aboard a plane with an all-male collection of passengers, mostly criminals, in northern Alaska when it crashes in a blizzard. He is immediately in the presence of a man whose guts have been torn out in the impact, is bleeding out and still talking.

> *The man screams, terrified:*
> *"What's happening to me? What's happening!"*
> *Ottway, in a surprisingly calm tone says simply,*
> *"Well, you're dyin', that's what's happening to ya."*
> *The man, in his same frantic tone, asks, "What do I do? What do I do!"*
> *"Just let it slide over you," says Ottway gently.*

One person helping another one die. A classic scene over the centuries; one that has precipitated much of the theology by which we calm ourselves in the face of life's greatest mystery—what's next after life is over? The twentieth century brought out two developments that improved that impulse to help one another let go of this life and approach the next world, if there is one. Hospice and palliative care have brought new human help to people in their last days and months than anything else in centuries. Approaching death rips away many of our trivial interests and petty concerns, almost forcing focus on "the hour of our death." [2]

The rapidly developing inter-disciplinary service of palliative care is, in itself, spiritual care. Its nature, as motivated by meeting, informing, partnering with, and bolstering the human spirits of very sick people, makes it a unique area of spiritual care. Born in medicine and often independent of religion, it takes a path more towards humanism, albeit honoring religion for its human value rather than excluding it. Like Alcoholics Anonymous, it emerged to fill a long-standing void in the ability of religion, medicine, government, and the behavioral sciences to adequately care for the human spirits of people in specifically difficult life situations. Palliative care developed in the last quarter of the 20th century to use interdisciplinary collaboration in new ways to care for people in the upheaval of facing very serious illness and dying.

Palliative care teams are generally organized around a medical practitioner, mostly physicians and nurse practitioners, as those who currently carry the professional and legal responsibilities of hospital admissions, official diagnosis, ordering the course of treatment, and writing notes that record the medical care. Juan Iregui is an internist physician with a degree in bioethics and twenty years of experience leading palliative care teams in New York,

Florida and Washington State and has spoken nationally on the intricacies of patient conversations in that service. He and his colleagues have developed highly successful palliative care frameworks that guide their care of patients and their relationships with attending and referring physicians.

Two case examples below illustrate common conversations they make in an ordinary workday, confronting patients about their unrealistic outcome expectations, and the physicians in charge of their care about the over-optimistic attitudes they often imply to their patients as they decline. Iregui works quietly and always empathetically to gradually improve the authenticity, interpersonal courage, and professional intimacy of those end-of-life conversations. He invites both sides of the patient-physician dialogue to simplify and clarify their interaction for better dying experiences on the one hand, and improved physician satisfaction on the other.

Confronting Patients and Families

A perennial project of most palliative care cases is managing expectations. As people get sicker with such conditions as heart failure or cancer, they decline. Maybe not rapidly or alarmingly, but relentlessly, overall. As they get worse, their realistic chances of recovery or even improvement typically grow dim. But for many, their positive expectations do not wane as fast as their health. They eventually arrive at a personal place in which their expectations remain unrealistically bright. At some point in their decline, they may benefit from communication that challenges those cheery or spartan expectations that once served them well, but now set them up for dying without personal and interpersonal preparations. About 75% want to be told when it becomes clear to medical practitioners around them that they are not going to be returned to enjoyable functioning. For various reasons, they often are not offered access to this important information.

Palliative care teams seek to get and keep a grasp on the inner expectations of patients as information about their illness gradually and sporadically becomes available. It is a team shared responsibility to elicit the thinking and attitudes of patients by candid questions, disclosing and describing new technical images and data, and careful listening. Iregui uses the phrase "we make the invisible, visible" in referring to this consultative relationship.

There is an art to this project of managing the changing expectations of patients. When there is serious bad news to be communicated, he uses a practical three-step-process he fashioned from reading clinicians' published wisdom[3] and his own considerable experience, to provide the information in the best form he can that is realistic—neither brutal honesty nor cheery optimism.

That approach starts with an early question to all palliative care patients about how they want to receive new information as it is generated in the development of the patient's illness so he and his team can tailor the conveying of the new information to the patient's preferences. Dr. Iregui asks every patient quite clearly and directly, some initial question like, "As more information becomes available about your condition, how do you want us to share it with you?"

From one point of view, he is "cleaning up" previous physicians' paucity of openness, thoroughness, communication skill and moral courage to tell the bad news in a way the patient and family are most likely to hear it. In stage-four cancer, for example, 40% of patients still believe that surgery could cure them. Iregui and his team are relentlessly seeking to get a realistic view to patients and keep them abreast of changes all along the way of their treatment.

When the first conclusive indication of irreversible decline emerges from image and lab data, that the patient has reached a medical situation from which they will most certainly not recover to any enjoyable life, it is time for the pivotal conversation with them. A process for confronting the patient about their now overly positive expectations has been developed by clinician-writers at Harvard and other places of innovation. Dr. Iregui has fashioned his own basic framework of how to approach that conversation with all of its possible variations.

His first step is already complete. Soon after initially meeting the patient, usually weeks or months earlier, he asks something like, "If the time comes that I will have to tell you seriously difficult new information about your condition, how would you like me to do that?" About 25% of patients do not want their physician to tell them the full truth about their condition, preferring them to tell a close relative or just write it in the chart they will never ask to see.

As part of his preparation, he also reminds himself to *detach from outcomes,* a skill he continues to develop. This allows him to direct his efforts to the process of disclosure and decision-making, trusting that a well-informed patient will make the right decision from his perspective even though at times he may disagree with their decision. Dying is as much a part of life as being born. Avoiding it until one can't anymore, and then embracing it with integrity, may be the best sign of maturity and a life well lived. He is doing his part in facilitating that process.

Also, in preparing himself, he re-familiarizes his memories of the course of the patient's illness, their personality, and what he knows of their values, hopes and dreams for the future, if any. He is getting clear in his own mind precisely what the patient's condition is. Iregui has a life commitment to finding an economy of accurate words with which to confront them, combining the stark truth with a kind attitude and voice tone that cannot be faked. It needs to be authentic, so he generates here-and-now compassion inside himself before the moments of encounter.

The second step is his telling the patient the new information with directness and calm precision, putting the most salient point upfront, not obfuscated by excessive medical jargon of good intentioned cheery tones. Iregui and other physicians have adopted from journalism the phrase, "Don't bury the headline!" Don't surround the serious news the patient needs to hear with positive, irrelevant facts, medical jargon or slender possibilities that often leave the patient confused or abandoned with "nobody tells me anything" attitudes. He is hyper-aware of how this patient's previous medical practitioners may have cushioned the truth at other stages of the illness and believes it is an ethical responsibility to convey accurate information in whatever way this person can hear it best. That is an aspect of the art of medicine that needs intuition and concentration and is inherently fraught with ambiguity. But as in painting and music, effort and repeated experience with reflection teach those open to continually learning.

The third step of Iregui's process is his response to the patient's initial reaction to the "serious news." After telling the patient in the way they have said they wanted new information to be made available to them, he waits in silence in the presence of the patient, observing their response or reaction, resisting the temptation to use more words to soften the impact and distract the patient from their own authentic inner processes. That interpersonal waiting may be the most important five to ten seconds of palliative care practice. The patient almost invariably responds to that brief but profound silence with directness about some form of their values, what is important to them at this pivotal moment in their lives. The doctor's response depends on the patient's reaction — whether emotional or cognitive.

If the patient's reaction is cognitive, such as a medical question, request for description of the manner of dying they will face, or seeking clarification of the new disclosure, the doctor's response is cognitive too, answering the question, providing further information, or guessing at the likely prognosis of pain or the likely experience of dying from the patient's specific illness. A supportive comment about commitment to future care, palliation of pain, or offers of religious/spiritual support may follow.

More often, the patient's first response to the serious news is some form of emotion, however. Then Iregui is ready with an empathetic response to the fear, anger, sadness, regret, or hurt, whichever comes across from the patient most clearly. Conveyed empathy still stands as the most human and caring attitude in spiritual care. It may be something spoken calmly like, "This is really hard," for example; or, "I can see this is very hard for you to hear," or, "I can see that this is really difficult for you." Some reassurance that there will be compassionate help along the way of the patient's future may follow in the next few minutes, but not so quickly that it is dismissive of the profundity of the moment. An offer of referral to spiritual leaders or social work connections is then not uncommon.

The important thing is the sustained presence of a savvy medical practitioner willing to respond freshly to the patient's lead. ("Sit" and "stay" would be the appropriate dog commands! Or, the Jewish proverb: Don't just do something, sit there). After the jolt of the bad news, patients benefit from some deep impression of the non-verbal care of a medically experienced person who understands and will give the time and presence it takes to incorporate the bad news into their life. That experience can be the most pivotal care experience of a lifetime. Canned speeches or pedantic teaching will likely be felt as abandonment. Dr. Iregui says, "You must always speak the truth but never separated from compassion."

Confronting Physicians

The grounding ethical and moral principle for physicians is faithfulness to the massive trust placed in them by a society that helped them gain that position of trust through public education. That trust injects a moral imperative on medical practitioners to function only in the best interest of the people they serve. *Beyond being a place of honor, an esteemed social role, and a lucrative profession, medicine is a binding responsibility to make all other influences and pressures secondary to the highest good of every single patient they serve.* That includes a fair amount of self-awareness in physicians as they joust with their own partially conscious motives, proclivities, and avoidances of unsavory aspects inherent in that role.

Palliative care physicians have a unique perspective from which to assess the communication of attending physicians with their patients. When they take a case at the request of a patient, family member, staff member or a physician, they can peruse the entire history of treatment in the medical record. It sometimes becomes apparent that a given physician has misled a patient and/or family about the seriousness of the medical issue, its prognosis, and the reasonable expectations of the patient and family member regarding any hope of quality recovery, i.e., there will be no returning to a previous level of health.

Dr. Iregui says he has only twice in his substantial career found a physician who exhibited intentional or seriously negligent behavior that needed intervention from regulatory agencies. But very frequently he has needed to confront a physician about ordinary negligence or unsatisfactory practice, medically or ethically.

Here is one of them he calls Dr. M.

Patient is a 47-year-old woman with Stage IV stomach cancer who is very motivated to receive any available treatments, in her words: "I want something done." Patient was initially scheduled to receive outpatient chemotherapy but had a blood clot that precipitated her hospitalization. Because of weight loss the oncologist documented on the chart that they had spoken to patient about hospice and that more treatments were not available.

When Palliative Medicine spoke to the patient, the patient stated that the oncologist told her that "if you get stronger, perhaps, we can look for other treatments."

Though common, that was a violation of professional responsibility. The oncologist had shared with other clinicians that he did not think the patient could get stronger and instead of being truthful, he gave her false hope. Clinicians are known to do this because they feel terrible telling patients the truth, since they are ill-equipped to deal with emotions and because they don't want to "take away hope."

Iregui then takes it upon himself to confront the oncologist about what is an apparent habit or pattern of communication that steals from dying people the opportunity to finish personal and interpersonal business, express a quality goodbye to people they really love, apologize for some behavior they regret, verbally forgive those people they once resented, and attend to financial and other material matters that tie up loose ends of a lifetime. His meeting with the oncologist is rather simple and he makes it easy. He never confronts without first finding common ground with the other person and without reminding himself to express empathy first. He calls it, "attributing positive intent," a phrase invented by management development experts meaning, assuming that a person is doing their best with the best of intentions in a uniquely complex situation in which they find themselves.

Iregui: "Hi Dr. M. I spoke with the patient and what she got from your conversation with her is that she needs to get stronger so she can have more chemotherapy. Is that what we should do, to encourage her to go to rehabilitation instead of considering hospice as you wrote in your note?"

Dr M: "Well, theoretically that is possible, but I don't think it is going to happen for her; she is too weak."

Iregui: "Did you share with her that you are worried, that this is as strong as she is going to get?"

Dr M: "I didn't want to take away her hope."

Iregui: "You know, false hope can be more devastating for patients and families because they don't get the opportunity to plan ahead, and end up missing opportunities to have closure with relatives, and to be surrounded by loved ones instead of going to a facility, trying to get stronger".

Dr. M: "What would be a better way to communicate with her?"

Iregui: "Would you want to try saying: My hope is that you do well and get stronger. I am worried though that this is as strong as you are going to get and I feel that getting hospice to help you get home to be with your family might be the best option."

Outcome: Dr Iregui wrote, "The oncologist went back and talked to the patient. I wasn't present, but I heard later during the day that the patient had chosen hospice."

The important point here is not the patient choosing hospice but proper disclosure from the physician. Once the physician fulfills his professional responsibility of being truthful, Iregui suggests that they are more likely to be able to let go of the outcome. Whether or not the patient chooses hospice is irrelevant, because if the patient declines hospice, they are doing it after *having access to the information that a prudent person would need to make an informed decision.*

The ingrained habit of many physicians, even today, is that while in possession of clear diagnostic data indicating that a patient will never again return to any acceptable level of enjoyable functioning, is to fill a few sentences with phrases and platitudes like, "There are still things we can try…," or, "You're really a trooper in this war against your cancer…," and in response to a patient's pensive question, "Don't you worry about that. Let me worry about that."

"That common habit is unethical," says Iregui. And he works daily to stem that tide, one colleague at a time.

Contact Info: Juan Iregui, MD, MA jciregui@iCloud com

[1] Carnahan, Joe, director. *The Grey*. Open Road Films, 2011.

[2] A famous phrase from a ritual prayer said fifty times in about fifteen minutes in the rosary, an ancient meditation tool devised as a substitute for reciting fifty Old Testament psalms by pilgrims to holy places in the third century. It distinguishes two separate and different times, "now" as juxtaposed to "the hour of our death."

[3] Anthony Back, Robert Arnold and James Tulsky, *Mastering Communication with Seriously Ill Patients: Balancing Honesty with Empathy and Hope. Cambridge* (New York: University Press, 2009)

Chapter Five:

God's Hands, Miracles, and the Good Fight
by
Amy Sanchez

Amy Sanchez is the Director of Chaplains at Children's Hospital of Orange County (CHOC) where she often meets with parents having difficulty accepting the deep sickness and serious injury of their children. Religious belief often bolsters them, but at times seems to hold back their acceptance of realistic outcomes. She and other hospital staff courageously and deftly manage their expectation, as they gradually move into acceptance of the terminal nature of their child's path. She begins with the questions that are a part of her everyday work and ministry. What is this person's spirituality? What is their faith tradition? What is their belief system, and is it helping or hurting their ability to cope, make decisions, and function in this chaos?

A chaplain worth their weight will dig deep in exploration to find even glimpses of insight into these questions. This is, of course, the work of spiritual assessment. So, what happens when a chaplain is met with answers that seem to point to a spiritual framework or a religious tradition; and yet, these resources seem to be at the very least impeding if not outright harming the individual's ability to cope or make decisions?

In the pediatric intensive care unit at the children's hospital where I have worked over the past four years, there are common theological concepts that are cited by parents and families in the moments, days, weeks and even months where they walk alongside their critically ill children and seek to make sense, find meaning, cope and most of all, draw on a belief system that may or may not make room for the reality presently staring them in the face.

"It's in God's Hands."

"We're waiting for a miracle."

"(S)he's a fighter."

In this ICU setting, we get these responses from parents all the time. So often, in fact, it becomes our work to make sure we do not just assume what the person saying them means. So, we probe. We pull the string to see how far they have followed these thoughts into their circumstances and how well they play out from start to finish.

In an ideal setting, parents have lived enough life to have had their belief systems challenged and they are familiar with pushing back, reimagining, and being uncomfortable with real life meeting conceptual spirituality. However, quite often, we see parents in what has been up to this point, the absolute worst nightmare they could imagine, and they are trying to piece together all the things they have heard in the past or told themselves they believe without weighing their veracity. Moreover, sometimes parents will even cling to statements like these to stall the medical team, delay the decision-making process, or even to relinquish themselves from their own agency in their current set of circumstances in the name of mysterious spirituality, religion and beliefs.

Why does it matter?

On so many levels this matters. To hide behind a spiritual or religious belief to avoid, delay or prolong the inevitable is more harmful than helpful. The work of the chaplain, as part of the inter-disciplinary team, is to take her assessment to the team and help them understand what the barriers for the parents are and why they are there. It is the chaplain's role to come up with a plan of care to help the parents press into their beliefs in a way that hopefully will generate agency, comfort, hope and movement. In an ideal situation, the chaplain is able to facilitate this journey. However, that is not always the case. Sometimes, it becomes important for the chaplain to be able to articulate this to the Interdisciplinary Team (IDT), that just as there are limits of care for the medical team, there are also limits to the care that the chaplain can provide. If the parents are not willing to go on the journey, it is not the chaplain's job to convince them, fix them, or "work her magic."

This is especially important when the chaplain sees other factors outside the realm of spiritual care at work. For example, we've noticed that the parents' attachment styles often dictate their response to their child's condition and the possible outcomes. We have tested this out with our psychology colleagues and have agreed that often, a parent with secure attachments from childhood, or relearned in adulthood, tend to have more secure attachments to the divine or a God-like figure, their beliefs, religion, etc. Conversely, those with anxious, avoidant, or disorganized attachment styles tend to have views of God, religion and spirituality informed by their complicated attachments.[1] This can provide a barrier, limiting the care the chaplain can provide if the parents are unwilling or unable to explore what is at the root of their perspectives and what informs those roots.

We had a patient in the PICU who had been with us for several months. Within the first thirty days it was apparent to the medical team that this patient would not recover and that to continue care would just prolong the inevitable, and in such a way that would cause tremendous suffering to the patient, the family and the team.

So, our team did what our team does so brilliantly: They spoke in compassionate yet certain terms about what they could expect and what the road ahead would look like for their beloved child. The family held "strong" Christian faith and told the chaplain that it was all "in God's hands." As the chaplain explored what this meant to the mother, he began to wonder if this was perhaps one way she could rid herself of the unspeakable burden of having to make medical decisions that no parent *should* ever have to make. The chaplain pressed deeper, and the mother stated that if her daughter's lung capacity dropped to a certain percentage, she would take that as a sign and make the necessary decisions to move forward.

However, it was not a question of if this would happen, rather, when would it happen. So, when it did happen, mom decided that it was "still in God's hands" and that her daughter was a fighter. As the chaplain continued to journey with mom, his suspicions were confirmed. Her beliefs were functioning as a bypass. If it is in God's hands, and my daughter is a fighter, then I must take a wait-and-see approach.

There was another family whose son was actually a fighter, trained in boxing. The prognosis for this patient, again, was bleakly eminent. As the chaplain dialogued with this father, the father used boxing as a metaphor for his son's ability to fight, persevere and win the battle. The chaplain delicately forged ahead with this dad, asking difficult questions and probing for what was informing this from a spiritual perspective. Of course, it wasn't long before dad quoted I Timothy 6:12, to explain that his son was "fighting the good fight." The irony of this is that if we read on, the author of this passage instructs us to take hold of the eternal life, which God has called us to. But so often, in our moments of crisis, we stop at fighting the good fight, because what does it mean to quit fighting?

The chaplain skillfully elaborated on the boxing metaphor and called to attention that sometimes, in the boxing arena, the coach decides enough is enough and "throws in the towel." It is an act of mercy, grace, love, and compassion. This conversation led the chaplain to realize this dad did not just see his son as fighting the good fight; he also was fighting right alongside with him. The chaplain then realized, it was the son that needed to be the one to throw in the towel, if only he could.

There was another situation where two families were in the PICU the same weekend, whose children had both drowned. Both families were going through the same series of tests, both patients were progressing to brain death, both outcomes were bleak.

One family who identified themselves as Protestant Christians immediately inquired about organ donation. The parents seemed to have a healthy and supportive relationship with one another, their family and community. Their faith made room for this loss and they believed they could make meaning and give purpose to their child's life through organ donation.

The other family, who identified as Roman Catholic and had strong Catholic beliefs, chose another route. They refused to "give up on their child" and they were "waiting for a miracle." The parents were estranged from one another. The relationship between the mother and the grandmother was volatile and the extended family exhibited high conflict. Their beliefs told them to "never give up" and that miracles happen.

The medical team was perplexed at how two families could be in the exact same circumstances and come to two completely different conclusions. This speaks to the diversity in beliefs, interpretation of scriptures, and probably even more so, the attachment styles at play in these circumstances. One family saw the miracle in being able to give life to several other humans by laying down the life of their own precious child. Another family could only see the miracle in the healing and recovery of their precious child.

Is one belief right and one wrong? Probably not for any of us to decide. But the way I see it as a chaplain, is that it is my job to assess whether the beliefs that are informing the thoughts, feelings and actions of our families is helping them or harming them. If these beliefs are in fact harmful, is there a way that I can help them navigate, reframe, reimagine a thought pattern that still falls within their spiritual framework while becoming helpful to them; they are coping, they can grasp and interact with reality, they can ask and answer the "what if" questions.

We had an immigrant family whose son was instrumental in helping them launch and maintain their family business and who also led them to their Christian faith. His decline became eminent during passion week. The parents were struggling to make medical decisions that would end their son's suffering rather than prolong it. The chaplain and I discussed the timing of passion week and bringing in the passion narrative, reminding the family that the promise is life in eternity for everyone. After all, the Christian faith believes that death does not have the final say (John 11:26). To everyone's shock, the parents believed, as many Christians do, that their son was suffering as Christ suffered and that there was no amount of suffering that would be too great if it meant he would pull through. This particular statement was quite distressing on the medical team, and they looked to the chaplain to help make sense of it all.

In so many of these cases, ethics consults are called, family conferences are held, multi-specialty meetings are held, and the team is forced to address the professed spiritualty at play: Is it a barrier to care? Is there an ethical dilemma? Why can't the chaplain just fix it?

Often, as chaplains, we can be tempted to feel like failures or to feel ineffective when we cannot help the parents make the turn. This is when it is helpful to remind ourselves, and those with whom we work closely, that spiritually presupposes a psychology, and there is often so much more underneath the stated belief system with which we are working. Indoctrination, trauma, individuality, attachments, generational patterns, etc. all play a role in how we, as humans, leverage our spiritual beliefs and practices.

For many, this means trying to fit a square peg into a round hole

Ideally, the chaplain can make inroads and forward movement. But these are examples in which medical teams are forced to face the dilemma of providing "futile" care in the name of faith: "God's hands," "miracles," and "fighting the good fight."

Then the work of the chaplain shifts to care and support for the team, bringing insight, explanation and hopefully some added context for them regarding the parents' process and how expressed religion, spirituality and belief systems are unique to each individual expressing them and are always presupposed by psychology. Sometimes, it becomes important for the chaplain to remind the IDT, that just as there are limits of care for the medical team, there are also limits to the care that the chaplain can provide.

If the parents are not willing to go on the journey, it is not the chaplain's job to convince them, fix them or "work her magic." Sometimes, there is only so much a chaplain can do with "it's in God's hands."

Contact Info: Amy Sanchez, MDiv, Manager of Spiritual Care – Children's Hospital of Orange County, Orange, CA asanchez@choc.org

[1] Pehr Granqvist, *Religion and Spirituality: A Wider View* (New York: The Guilford Press, 2020), chapter 3 in attachment.

Chapter Six:

The Previously Traumatized: Confrontation in the Context of Trauma-Informed Care
by
Rabbi Beth Naditch

Trauma changes its victims and reshapes their lives. How then does a caregiver use the intervention of confrontation with the millions of people who have been previously traumatized? The developing practice of trauma informed care has addressed this question, and Rabbi Naditch here describes some ways in which spiritual caregivers can take traumatization in consideration in their work.

The U.S. Health and Human Services Administration defines individual trauma as resulting from *"an event, series of events, or set of circumstances that is experienced by an individual as physically or emotionally harmful or life threatening and that has lasting adverse effects on the individual's functioning and mental, physical, social, emotional, or spiritual well-being."* [1]

When Mara[2] walked into the classroom one late June morning, she had deep shadows under her eyes, her complexion was gray, and she looked stricken. I assumed something terrible had happened in her personal life and asked if everything was okay. "I need to talk to you in private," she whispered. Concerned, I ushered her into my office and offered her a chair, preparing internally for what she might have to share. Eyes downcast, she began to speak haltingly. "I wasn't able to finish my theological reflection last night." Having braced myself from her appearance to hear about a breakup with her partner, a death or an illness, I was greatly relieved.

"Okay, life happens sometimes, I'm sure there was a reason," I told her. "When we read the reflections out loud during our group, you can either choose to share a few thoughts verbally, or we can have you share yours at a future date." Her head snapped up, confusion and relief playing across her features. "You mean I don't have to leave the program? But I didn't do the assignment, and I let everyone down."

Clearly, Mara was expecting a severe consequence for a slight misstep, and even more clearly, had suffered some earlier trauma in schooling or previous work environments. The inner monologue with which she had already confronted herself likely contained echoes of that trauma, and was far more severe than anything I might have even considered saying. The relief in Mara's eyes reminded me of an older book title written for adults with ADHD: "You mean I'm not lazy, stupid, or crazy?"[3] While her response to not meeting an obligation was slightly more extreme than some, I have experienced a version of that same terror in many students and staff, who have trauma in their backgrounds. My approach is to be fully present for such people in a way that can strengthen their resilience. Only someone who is available for learning will be able to receive feedback, and only someone who feels safe (enough) will be able to hear any kind of challenge or confrontation.

Perhaps my favorite definition of resilience comes from the Center for Child Study at Harvard University. They write, *"The essence of resilience is a positive, adaptive response in the face of significant adversity. It is neither an immutable trait nor a resource that can be used up. On a biological level, resilience results in healthy development because it protects the developing brain and other organs from the disruptions produced by excessive activation of stress response systems. Stated simply, resilience transforms potentially toxic stress into tolerable stress."*[4]

Research has shown that resilience is primarily built in the context of relationship,[5] which should guide our approach to confrontation with those who have trauma in their background or who are currently in a state of traumatic activation.

Using the language of Laurent Daloz, the ideal relationship between a CPE Educator and student, or between a caring work supervisor and staff member, is a kind of "holding environment," a safe context in and out of which a person grows.[6] Only when trust is present will people allow themselves to be vulnerable, and only then will they be truly available to hear the care underneath confrontation.[7] He writes that the mentoring relationship is about "engendering trust and nurturance—caring for growth. Teaching is thus preeminently an act of care." [8] With only trust and support, however, there is little impetus for growth in a mentoring environment. For this reason, I seek that sweet spot of balance between support and challenge of students and staff in cases of confrontation. Too much support with too little challenge, and a person might remain contented, and feel safe, but will remain static. It would not ultimately be in their best interests to not challenge them to grow. Too much challenge with too little support, and anxiety is too high, creating an environment where a person is unavailable to engage with the confrontation. The right balance of support and challenge creates a holding environment which allows students and staff to take risks.

Perhaps the most central tenet of confrontation in a context of trauma-informed care is that it should take place in the context of a trusting relationship. People with trauma backgrounds may be slower to trust, especially if coming from a background of a minority or marginalized group whose trauma has not been recognized. Trust must be built by careful attunement to students, patients, or staff. The one offering challenge must be attuned to working styles, learning styles, cultural narratives, and individual stories of those on the receiving end of challenge or confrontation. Moreover, the potential confronter should model trustworthiness and safety through being transparent, reliable, non-shaming, and building safety through easily accessible information.[9] Trust is not immediate, and it is necessary. It takes time to build and support.

Returning to Mara, it turned out that the assignment, *a theological reflection on safety*, had activated some old trauma from her family of origin. This, blended with a history of being punished in school for undiagnosed learning disabilities, had left her in an activated and frozen state where she was neither able to complete the assignment nor to sleep. She chose to share with the group that she had not completed the assignment because it brought up some "old wounds," and was received generously by her peers. I celebrated that she had taken a major step by even showing up that day, which was outside of her usual pattern of running away when she experienced herself as a failure. Her trust was building slowly but surely, and by the end of the CPE unit, she was able to engage with non-defensive presence when a peer confronted her about an off-handed comment she had made which had hurt the peer's feelings.

Steven Hobfoll and Patricia Watson have identified five central areas which create a holding environment for one who is suffering from stress injury, or even more severely, trauma: *safety, calm, connection, hope, and self-efficacy*.[10] In Mara's story, we have seen how creating safety through trust-building, connection, and calm reactions led to the possibility of her surviving—and thriving in a context where confrontation was growth-full.

Another case of necessary confrontation which used these concepts was the family situation in our rehabilitation unit. Aaron Breakstone was an 86-year-old retired pediatrician who was well known in his community for the excellent care he gave to generations of children and their families. In addition to his professional role, Dr. Breakstone was involved in his local synagogue and had been on several boards of local social justice organizations. He was known for his tireless dedication to his patients and causes. Dr. Breakstone's wife, Emily, was admitted to the rehabilitation unit of our chronic care hospital for care after a recent surgery and Dr. Breakstone, who was described as "very loving and strong advocate" for his wife in her admission notes, wanted to keep an eagle eye on her care. He explained to staff that he would move into Emily's room with her 24/7.

A cot was procured by one of his daughters and set up in his wife's room. It became clear very quickly that Dr. Breakstone's advocacy was interfering with his wife's care. The room was too crowded with his cot, he himself was a fall risk, and he would object to therapeutic assessments and interventions (such as physical therapy) if he felt that Emily was "too tired" to engage at that moment. Staff were getting frustrated, as they were thwarted in their treatment of their patient and tried to ask him to move out of the room. But each time the subject was broached, Dr. Breakstone would dig in and redouble his efforts to watch over his wife attentively. It became clear that Dr. Breakstone was exhibiting behaviors classic for trauma survivors. It is important to note here that trauma is not necessarily restricted to a distinct event but is related to the degree of helplessness which is felt in the highly stressful situation.

Going back to the definition of trauma at the beginning of this chapter, *trauma results from an event, series of events, or set of circumstances experienced by an individual as physically or emotionally harmful or life threatening.* He was attempting to self-soothe by taking steps for self-efficacy by moving into his wife's room, but this was backfiring. Confrontation was necessary, and the team needed to exercise great care in their methods.

After a week, a family meeting was called with the goal of removing Dr. Breakstone from his wife's room outside of normal day visiting hours. The interdisciplinary team met beforehand to strategize messaging. Two chaplains, one of whom was known to Dr. Breakstone through his community work, were invited to the meeting to offer a trusted and familiar presence (safety and connection), joining the physician, social worker, nurse manager, occupational therapist, physical therapist, Dr. Breakstone, Emily Breakstone, and their two adult daughters.

Dr. Sandra Bloom suggests that cultivating curiosity about the person experiencing traumatic stress is key.[11] Blaustein and Kinniburgh[12] offer a roadmap of questions to consider from this curious stance:

- What might this person be reacting to?

- What might this person need?

- What might they be trying to tell me?

- How can I keep this person safe?

- How can I keep myself safe?

- What can I do to help this person regain a sense of safety or control?

Ideally, we wanted to try and help Dr. Breakstone stay inside the resilient zone, where people experience the best capacity for flexibility, pro-social behavior, executive functioning, and being responsive rather than reactive.[13] At the meeting, each member of the multi-disciplinary team tried an approach from their field. Difficult information about Emily's condition and her need for unimpeded treatment was shared as gently as possible, but Dr. Breakstone appeared more agitated. Dr. Laurie Leitch notes that *"every individual is wired with defensive responses (Fight, Flight, Freeze, and Tend and Befriend) that can be automatically and unconsciously triggered by even the perception of threat. This appraisal of threat takes place initially below the level of consciousness and is entirely subjective."*[14] Dr. Breakstone was stuck in "fight," with his perception that he would be denied access to his wife and operating outside of the resilient zone.

Tensions remained high, until the chaplain revisited these questions: "What might this person be reacting to?" What might this person need? What might they be trying to tell me?"

She asked "Can you tell us about why it is important to you to be Emily's primary caregiver?"

At this point the floodgates opened, and Dr. Breakstone began to cry. "In my adult life, I know that I chose my career and community work over family, and I feel terrible about my choices. Yes, I did good in the world, but I abandoned Emily and my children at times when they needed me, and I left her alone to basically keep our home running. I got all the glory, but she was always in the background making it possible for me to do what I did. I didn't appreciate her enough and now she is failing. I owe it to her to make up for all the times I wasn't present, and I vowed to myself that when I retired, I would be with her to meet her every need."

This was the breakthrough we needed. Dr. Breakstone felt safe enough and connected enough to the team to share his story. The physician, exuding a calm presence, gently explained to Dr. Breakstone that Emily needed more care than he himself could provide, and recommended the best way to meet her needs would be to allow the medical team to care for her, so he could stay in his role as attentive, loving, and supportive husband. In doing so, she gave him another path towards self-efficacy and hope, by redirecting his efforts towards a useful and needed role.

Even before the COVID-19 global pandemic, we knew that trauma was pervasive in health care and education. We were aware that most clients/patients/recipients of services in the mental health system are trauma survivors. We know that most American elders of this generation have some trauma history, based on their generation's living through wars, the Depression, possible immigration, and personal events. We are increasingly aware as a society of historical trauma, racial trauma, epigenetic trauma, and developmental trauma. With the stress of the past two years of pandemic life, we can safely assume that confrontation with all those around us should be undertaken with an awareness of trauma-informed care, and in as growth promoting and healing a way as possible.

Contact Info: Rabbi Beth Naditch, PhD, ACPE Certified Educator, Hebrew Senior Life/Hebrew Rehabilitation Center, Boston, MA benaditch@gmail.com

[1] Substance Abuse and Mental Health Services Administration (SAMHSA), "Concept of Trauma and Guidance for a Trauma-Informed Approach," HHS Publication No. (SMA) 14-4884. Rockville, MD: 2014, 7. https://store.samhsa.gov/system/files/sma14-4884.pdf (accessed January, 2022).

[2] All names used in this chapter are pseudonyms and identifying features of stories have been altered to protect the privacy of patients, families, and students.

[3] Kate Kelly and Peggy Ramundo, *You Mean I'm Not Lazy, Stupid, or Crazy: A Classic Self-Help Book for Adults with ADHD* (New York: Simon and Schuster, 1996).

[4] National Scientific Council on the Developing Child, "Supportive Relationships and Active Skill-Building Strengthen the Foundations of Resilience," Working Paper 13, 2015. 1http://www.developingchild.harvard.edu

[5] National Scientific Council, ibid, 7.

[6] Laurent Daloz, *Effective Teaching and Mentoring: Realizing the Transformational Power of Adult Learning Experiences* (San Francisco: Jossey-Bass, 1986), 215.

[7] Parker Palmer, *A Hidden Wholeness* (San Francisco: Jossey-Bass, 2004), 58. A favorite passage of mine that speaks to this comes from Parker Palmer. He writes: "The soul, despite its toughness, is also essentially shy—just like a wild animal. It will flee from the noisy crowd and seek safety in the deep underbrush. If we want to see a wild animal, we know the last thing we should do is go crashing through the woods yelling for it to come out! But if we will walk into the woods quietly and sit at the base of a tree, breathing with the earth and fading into our surroundings, the wild creature we seek may eventually show up."

[8] Daloz, 237.

[9] In a work context, that could mean clarity of policies and expectations or a clear schedule. In a CPE or training context, it could mean an organized curriculum and calendar and clear expectations of requirements.

[10] Stevan E. Hobfoll et al. *Five Essential Elements of Immediate and Mid-Term Mass Trauma Intervention: Empirical Evidence* (Psychiatry, 2007) 70 (4): 283-315

[11] Sandra Bloom, "An Elephant in the Room: The Impact of Traumatic Stress on Individuals and Groups," http://www.sanctuaryweb.com/Portals/0/Bloom%20Pubs/2009%20Bloom%20An%20Elephant%20in%20the%20Room.pdf

[12] American Reading Company curriculum, Margaret Blaustein and Kristin Kinniburgh

[13] Leitch, L, "Action steps using ACEs and trauma-informed care: a resilience model," *Health Justice 5*, 5 (2017). https://doi.org/10.1186/s40352-017-0050 6-7

[14] Leitch, ibid, 7

Chapter Seven:

Sapphire Dignified:
Resisting the Angry Black Woman Motif in CPE Supervision
by
The Rev Dr Danielle J Buhuro

Racism as a societal blight has re-emerged in the public view, inspiring a host of initiatives to address and, in time, heal it. In this chapter, the author of Spiritual Care in an Age of Black Lives Matter, addresses the matter of unconscious bias in clinical pastoral education. With context and comment, she places us solidly at the center of how difficult confrontation can be in cross-cultural care.

Mandalyn Samson (name changed to honor confidentiality) was a middle-aged African American clergy woman. She had previously completed a unit of CPE at another ACPE-accredited center. Mandalyn felt a divine call to pursue a career in healthcare chaplaincy. While she was a very bright woman who had attended one of the nation's premier seminaries and was a well-respected clergy in her Christian denomination with decades of ministry experience, Mandalyn applied to four residency positions and was denied, being informed later that particular "red flag" language utilized in her first unit supervisory evaluation had stamped a black spot on future supervisors' inclinations to accept her into residency programs even despite her eagerness to learn, her well-kept professional persona, and her articulate command of research-based, inclusive and interreligious pastoral care vernacular in spiritual care encounters with patients.

What demonstrative words had her first unit supervisor, a European American older woman, donned in Mandalyn's first unit supervisory evaluation? The supervisory document included such language as "student is defensive,"; "hard to get along with"; "expresses inappropriate anger"; "centers only on her feelings and no one else's"; "resistant" and "angry". These words subsequently stifled Mandalyn's chances to succeed and obtain future units of CPE.

When Mandalyn's application arrived to me at my office door, I took a chance on Mandalyn and invited her to an interview for an open resident position at my institution. When I asked Mandalyn to expound on why her supervisor would use such language in the supervisory evaluation, Mandalyn drew attention to her innate sense of social justice in calling out racist incidents that she experienced occurring in the group and, as a result, these inflammatory words being used in the supervisory evaluation as retribution.

I accepted Mandalyn into the residency program at my healthcare institution, where she became very successful and greatly sought after as a soothing pastoral presence in the clinic. I affirmed Mandalyn's well-groomed pastoral gifts, skills and talents in my supervisory evaluations of Mandalyn's second, third, fourth and fifth units of CPE.

After the residency program ended, Mandalyn successfully landed a full-time, senior staff position at a Level I trauma center. Her life is subsequently different now. What if no other supervisor had given her a chance after her first unit of CPE to show that her first unit supervisor was racially biased, unaware and insensitive to historical cultural dynamics, and had inappropriately weaponized the first unit evaluation?

What Mandalyn has experienced in her first unit of CPE is not an isolated incident. Since the development of this "Angry Black woman" trope, African American women have had to work hard to resist demonstrating public displays of anger for fear of being dismissed as the "angry Black woman" or Sapphire stereotype. This stereotype began during the period of African Enslavement in the United States from 1619 to 1865 and was a cultural production of evil.

The Invention of 'Mammy': White Supremacy's Cultural Production of Evil

She nursed "nearly all of the children in the family" and was a "second mother." These were the words that a white elite Floria family used to describe their Black house slave, Mauma Mollie upon her death in the 1850's.[1] Years earlier, Mauma was illegally kidnapped from her home on the continent of Africa, like millions of other African bodies from 1619 to 1865, and viciously transported like used cargo to South Carolina. She would later again experience moral, emotional and physical displacement once more when she was transported like an animal to Jefferson County, Florida after being purchased by John and Eliza Partridge in the 1830's. It was at this moment that Mauma transformed into Mammy. Mauma, now serving as Mammy, would endure the internal psychological pain of emotional cutoff from her family of origin as well as an enslaved enmeshment to a white God-fearing Christian family while yet in still being regarded by the Partridge Family upon her death as "Black of skin but pure of heart, she doubtless stands among the faithful on the right of the King." [2]

Mauma's Mammy archetype was created by white supremacy during the period of African Enslavement (1619-1865) in these so-called United States of America. While many institutions, such as the Equal Justice Initiative in Montgomery, Alabama, place much emphasis on the kidnapping, terrorizing, segregation and mass incarceration of Black bodies, I contend that during African Enslavement in the U.S., white supremacy's most oppressive act has been its hand in creating culture about Black bodies. During African Enslavement, white Christian slave masters, with the intent to birth white supremacy, sought several means to justify the enslavement of African and African American bodies as a fundamental characteristic of the culture of the United States.

According to Merriam-Webster, culture is defined as:

> 1. The customary beliefs, social forms, and material traits of a racial, religious, or social group also: the characteristic features of everyday existence (such as diversions or a way of life) shared by people in a place or time popular *culture* Southern *culture*

2. The set of shared attitudes, values, goals, and practices that characterizes an institution or organization, e.g., a corporate *culture* focused on the bottom line

3. The set of values, conventions, or social practices associated with a particular field, activity, or societal characteristic studying the effect of computers on print *culture,* changing the *culture* of materialism will take time, Peggy O'Mara

4. The integrated pattern of human knowledge, belief, and behavior that depends upon the capacity for learning and transmitting knowledge to succeeding generations [3]

With this definition of culture in mind, good Christian slavemasters sought to demonstrate how African Enslavement was an intrinsic "value" to American culture, because it was a "convention, or social practice associated with a particular field, activity, or societal characteristic [of America's being and functioning]". White slavemasters desired to exhibit how African Enslavement was an intricate part of American culture by also highlighting how the enslavement of dark bodies was a "shared attitude, value, goal, and practice that characterizes an institution or organization [America]". Thus, white slavemasters worked hard to teach their children how important and necessary African Enslavement was to retain as a part of American culture because the process of teaching their future generations this phenomenon represented how "the integrated pattern of human knowledge, belief, and behavior that depends upon the capacity for learning and transmitting knowledge to succeeding generations."

White supremacy not only sought to define what is culture for the United States as a nation, but also unashamedly and unapologetically sought to define what is culture for Africans Americans as a particular racial group. With the above stated definition of culture from Merriam-Webster in mind, white supremacy has intentionally influenced how non-Africans and non-African Americans see the racial and ethnic "customary beliefs, social forms and material traits" of African and African American people in particular. White supremacy even goes as far as shaping how African and African American people themselves internalize feelings of shame, guilt and self-hatred about their own racial and ethnic "customary beliefs, social forms, and material traits."

While white slavemasters earnestly believed that African Enslavement was a part of American culture, as they defined culture, these men employed a particular methodological strategy to prove it: use of media. White supremacy has shaped African American culture through the use of media -specifically, movies, television shows, radio, books, postcards, newspapers, magazines and art. White supremacy uses these media outlets to shape African American culture as theologically sinful, psychologically unintelligent, morally unethical and anthropologically undeserving of basic human rights.

To justify African Enslavement, white Christian slavemasters meticulously and methodically created one stereotypical image of the African and African American woman as that of a Mammy. Slavemasters defined the culture of Black Women Mammies as having a "customary belief, attitude, or value" that was intrinsically happy and content with being enslaved. After African Enslavement, as the country moved towards the period of Jim Crow (1865-1950s), cinema on the Big Screen was used to further create fantasy. In these movies, Mammy carries particular characteristics other than simply being happy about being enslaved.

Mammy was created as being whom Townes calls "the evil twin" of the over-sexualized Jezebel.[4] Hattie McDaniel, the most popular Mammy figure in America's film history, played a character literally named "Mammy" in 1939's *Gone With The Wind*. McDaniel's Mammy character was a good, Christian God-fearing woman who was the epitome of the domesticated class. The character was a mothering figure above all who sacrificed loving her own children for the sake of loving her white family's children more. When given the opportunity to be free, the Mammy character resisted freedom and instead willingly chose to remain in captivity of the white family. McDaniel's Mammy was a physically large, overweight woman, as caricatured by the original Aunt Jemima syrup bottles, who struggled with health challenges. Mammy was always docile, subservient, and agreeable. She held a dark-skinned complexion.

According to Melissa Harris-Perry: "Unlike the bad black woman who was aggressively sexual, Mammy had no personal needs or desires. She was a trusted adviser and confidante whose skills were used exclusively in service of the white families to which she was attached. Mammy was not a protector or defender of black children or communities. She represented a maternal ideal, but not in caring for her own children. Her love, doting, advice, correction, and supervision were reserved exclusively for white women and children. Her loyal affection to white men, women, and children was entirely devoid of sexual desire." [5]

Gone With the Wind was not unique. These created Mammy characteristics ran rampant in other films, including:

Mammy as played by Jennie Lee in D. W. Griffith's 1915 silent epic *The Birth of a Nation*.

Aunt Dilsey, played by Hattie McDaniel, *Judge Priest*, 1934.

Louise Beavers played a mammy, cook, slave, or servant in almost all of her film roles. The more well-known are: *Imitation of Life* (1934), *Belle Starr* (1941), *Holiday Inn* (1942), *Jack London* (1943) and *I Dream of Jeanie* (1952).

Delilah, played by Virginia Capers, *Big Jake*, 1971

Ma Soupswill, Rare, *Grabbed by the Ghoulies*, 2003

Aunt Tempe, played by Hattie McDaniel, in *Song of the South*, 1946

These movies showcasing the Mammy produced or created a racist cultural perspective of Black women steeped in stereotypes. To oppress one individual is theologically defined as sin. However, to oppress an entire group of persons based on race, gender, class, sexual orientation, etc. is defined as evil. White supremacy's desire to develop or create racist tropes of Black women as Mammies through the use of media is, therefore, why Womanist Theologian Emilie Townes highlights the Mammy trope as a "cultural production of evil." [6] What is even most pervasive about the culturally produced Mammy is that she is a created fantasy inserted into the psyche of all of America's inhabitants alike. I assert that the reason Black women are primarily abused on social media is because white culture still desires for Black women to remain happy-go-lucky Mammies who are quiet and docile when instead many progressive, liberation-focused Black women speak truth to power, challenge oppression and push back against oppressive authorities, earning them the title of another stereotypical image created by white supremacy: The Despised Smart-Mouth, Emasculating Sapphire.

Still Desiring Mammy and Despising Sapphire: Labeling Black Women as "Angry" in CPE Group Life and Process

Who was "Sapphire"? According to Chanequa Walker-Barnes: "After slavery ended, the myth of Black women's promiscuity no longer played the same role in maintaining the economic and social order. And while the myth of the devoted, asexual servant was important to an economic system in which Black women were most frequently employed as domestic laborers in White households, by itself the Mammy image provided insufficient control over Black women's behavior. Thus, a third image—the matriarch—was born. The Mammy and the matriarch are closely related, but distinct in important ways.

"While the Mammy typifies the Black mother figure in white homes, the matriarch symbolizes the mother figure in black homes. Just as the Mammy represents the 'good' Black mother, the matriarch symbolizes the 'bad' Black mother." The matriarch is, in essence, "a failed Mammy." She possesses significant domestic skills and devotes much of her time to taking care of others. But her caregiving has a sharp edge. She is quick-tempered, aggressive, argumentative, domineering, unfeminine, and emasculating, particularly towards her Black male counterparts." [7]

I assert that the stereotypical image of Sapphire is implanted in the collective memory of America. Therefore, whenever America experiences a no-nonsense, progressive, self-actualized, liberated Black woman who courageously speaks out against injustice, the fantasized image of Sapphire arises in the consciousness of both white and Black America. Social media further instills this false memory and false identity. For a current example, one can turn to Congresswoman Maxine Waters and how she is attacked in digital space. "Kerosene Maxine", as she has been stereotypically nicknamed by former president Donald Trump, is white supremacy's present-day Sapphire. Maxine Waters is a not a passive Black woman, therefore white supremacy deems her identity as undesirable in stark contrast to Mammy. Why is this? This is because white supremacy, especially the former president, hates the democratic Congresswoman from California in that "Waters was one of the first Democrats in Washington to call for Trump's impeachment after his inauguration in 2016, calling him a scumbag, immoral, indecent and inhuman. She branded his staff the 'Kremlin Klan'." [8] Waters comments have been seen by white supremacists as "smart-mouthed" to and "emasculating" of the former male occupant of the Oval Office. Her presence is seen as a threat to the cultural status quo that white Christian slavemasters attempted to establish since the beginning of African Enslavement in 1619.

This dynamic is also true for Black female clergy in CPE learning environments who are seen as threats when they offer challenge in the Clinical Pastoral Education learning environment. CPE is an educational learning context whereby pastoral care students learn to claim and embrace their authentic feelings of sad, mad, scared, peaceful, joyful and powerful. When African American women enter the CPE learning process, many have no problem embracing and demonstrating these feelings except the feeling of mad for fear of being dismissed as the "angry Black woman" or Sapphire stereotype despite facilitating confrontation, challenge and accountability being integral aspects of the learning experience. This writer contends that redefining the character Sapphire with dignity can help African American female CPE students claim their own anger with dignity; and therefore, successfully enter into confrontation in the CPE group learning process. How do we supervise African American female students and allow them to challenge and confront dynamics in the group life and process without retribution and later labeling them as "angry"?

Inviting Confrontation Through an "Empathy-Education-Empowerment" Approach

I encourage educators to teach students what I have deemed an "Empathy-Education-Empowerment" approach to confrontation. First, students make an empathic statement about the person or event they'd like to confront or challenge. Learning occurs, first, through empathy. In my supervision with Mandalyn, I recognized an empathic presence beginning with the application and interview process of the program. I sensed her nervousness and anxiety when she called to inquire about the program and how to apply, wondering if I'd close the door on her given her first unit supervisor's final evaluation. After accepting Mandalyn into the program, I continued to extend her empathy during the beginning phase, or orientation, of the program. As the supervisor, I demonstrate empathy through what bell hooks terms as engagement.[9] By demonstrating engagement, Mandalyn internalized this as a key component of CPE and then modeled this empathy in the process of confrontation by first making an empathic statement about the person or event she wished to confront.

As the supervisor my role is to gently move the group to the next phase of the learning process. The next phase of the learning process is conflict/dominance/rebellion, according to Yalom.[10] During this phase, group members remove the masks or blinders and begin to relate to each other with honesty and integrity. I facilitate this process by modeling confrontation. I openly confronted Mandalyn in group about her pastoral growing edges. In turn, she began appropriately confronting her peer group members about their growing edges, as well as the growing edges of the group life and process. In the midst of this challenge and confrontation, education occurred.

Last but not least, my supervisory strategy empathizes empowerment. I believe students need empowerment to learn. This is because persons desire that their gifts, skills and talents are continuously affirmed. For example, when a student presents a verbatim, after employing empathy and education, the peer group and I make affirmative statements about the student's pastoral identity and competency. Receiving education or challenge without affirmation and empowerment is very difficult. If students receive education or challenge without affirmation and empowerment afterwards, then I believe they are left feeling exposed and vulnerable. Mandalyn demonstrated an ability to name an empowering statement to her peer group after giving confrontation and challenge.

By modeling empathy, education and empowerment in my own supervisory practice with Mandalyn and the peer group, I mirrored for the peer group that appropriate confrontation and challenge is healthy for the group process. I also mirrored for the group that when Mandalyn enters into confrontation, in between extending empathy and empowerment, the peer group does not have to feel threatened, and subsequently will not label Mandalyn as "angry." Another learning is that when I, as the supervisor, can receive confrontation and challenge from Mandalyn without labeling her as "angry," I directly foster dignity within Mandalyn and indirectly foster dignity within the larger cultural stereotypical Sapphire trope.

Sapphire Dignified

To tell persons, especially Black women, to resist experiencing anger is disrespectful, unhealthy and racially biased in the CPE learning experience. While we may not want to admit it, anger is real. Anger is not a feeling one can simply pray about, meditate away or ignore. This would be synonymous with sweeping it under the rug, but it's still there! Anger is an authentic, genuine feeling.

All persons experience anger without regard to race, gender, sexual orientation, class, etc., according to marriage and family therapist Dr. Gloria Willcox.[11] There are six major feelings all persons experience which Willcox creatively graphed on a Feeling Wheel.[12] Those feelings are "sad", "mad", "scared", "peaceful", "joyful" and "powerful." Western civilization believes that feelings can hold a level of currency. Some feelings are valued as right while other feelings are deemed wrong. African-centered psychologist Linda James Myers highlights Western civilization's goal to foster a dichotomous split between right and wrong feelings. Feelings of "sad", "mad", and "scared" are deemed as bad or negative whereas feelings of "peaceful", "joyful" and "powerful" are deemed as good and positive. Eastern civilization, however, highlights how there is no such dynamic as right or wrong feelings.[13]

Acknowledgement and affirmation of African American female student's anger in the supervisory process grants dignity and restores hope. This is because when one refuses to acknowledge "sad", "mad" or "scared" feelings that another experiences, one facilitates a disconnection within the other, leading the other to wrestle with anxiety, low self-esteem and depression, according to African psychologist Na'im Akbar.[14] This dynamic will foster indefinite feelings of dissatisfaction and others will constantly seek external validation to no avail, leading to perfectionism struggles later that can foster an internal implosion. Hopefully, we can all agree that society doesn't need any more extra implosions in vulnerable people.

Contact Info: The Rev Dr Danielle Buhuro, DMin, ACPE Certified Educator/Author, Sankofa CPE Center, Chicago, IL Daniel.Buhuro@AdvocateHealth.com

[1] Portrait of Mauma Mollie-1850 (png image), Library of Congress, https://www.loc.gov/item/2021669924

[2] Ibid.

[3] "culture." Merriam-Webster.com. 2011. https://www.merriam-webster.com

[4] Emilie M. Townes, *Womanist Ethics and the Cultural Production of Evil* (New York: Palgrave Macmillan, 2006), 31.

[5] Chanequa Walker-Barnes, *Too Heavy A Yoke — Black Women and the Burden of Strength* (Eugene, Cascade Books), 85

[6] Townes, ibid, 159

[7] Walker-Barnes, ibid, 88

[8] Rory Carroll, "You Better Shoot Straight: how Maxine Waters became Trump's public enemy No 1", TheGuardian.com, July 7, 2018

[9] bell hooks, *Teaching To Transgress: Education as he Practice of Freedom* (New York: Routledge, 1984).

[10] Irvin D.Yalom and Molyn Leszcz, *The Theory and Practice of Group Psychotherapy*, 5th Edition (New York: Basic Books, 2020), 314.

[11] Willcox, Gloria. "The Feeling Wheel: A Tool for Expanding Awareness of Emotions and Increasing Spontaneity and Intimacy." *Transactional Analysis Journal,* vol. 12, no. 4, 1982, 274–276, doi:10.1177/036215378201200411.

[12] Willcox, ibid.

[13] Linda James Myers, *Understanding an Afrocentric World View: Introduction to an Optimal Psychology* (Dubuque: Kendall Hunt Publishing, 1988).

[14] Na'im Akbar, *Akbar Papers in African Psychology* (Tallahassee: Mind Productions & Associates, 2003)

Bibliography

"A High-Tech Lynching," History News Network. Accessed June 9, 2021. https://historynewsnetwork.org/article/170071.

Burns, Janet. "Black Women Are Besieged On Social Media, And White Apathy Damns Us All." *Forbes Magazine,* March 19, 2019. https://www.forbes.com/sites/janetwburns/2017/12/27/black-women-are-besieged-on-social-media-and-white-apathy-damns-us-all/?sh=390eeda9423e.

Cone, James H. *The Cross and the Lynching Tree* (Maryknoll, NY: Orbis Books, 2019).

"culture." Merriam-Webster. Merriam-Webster. Accessed 9 June 2021. https://www.merriam-webster.com/dictionary/culture.

William Cummings, "Trump Slams 'Low IQ' Rep. Maxine Waters Who Called for Harassment of White House Officials," USA Today. Gannett Satellite Information Network, June 26, 2018.

https://www.usatoday.com/story/news/politics/onpolitics/2018/06/25/maxine-waters-trump-exchange/732505002/.

"Donald Trump Slams Maxine Waters After She Comments on Death Threats," Time, July 3, 2018. https://time.com/5329118/president-trump-maxine-waters-death-threat/.

Justin Doom, "Some women are attacked on Twitter every 30 seconds," Amnesty International, ABC News Network. Accessed 9 June 2021. https://abcnews.go.com/Technology/women-attacked-twitter-30-seconds-amnesty-international/story?id=59903343.

Elizabeth Dwoskin and Nitasha Tiku, "A Recruiter Joined Facebook to Help It Meet Its Diversity Targets. He Says Its Hiring Practices Hurt People of Color," The Washington Post. WP Company, April 9, 2021. https://www.washingtonpost.com/technology/2021/04/06/facebook-discrimination-hiring-bias/.

"Facebook and Instagram to Examine Racist Algorithms," BBC News, July 22, 2020. https://www.bbc.com/news/technology-53498685.

Stan Grant, "Black Writers Courageously Staring Down the White Gaze – This Is Why We All Must Read Them," The Guardian News and Media, December 31, 2015. https://www.theguardian.com/commentisfree/2015/dec/31/black-writers-courageously-staring-down-the-white-gaze-this-is-why-we-all-must-read-them.

History.com Editors, "Emmett Till is Murdered," History.com, A&E Television Networks, February 9, 2010. https://www.history.com/this-day-in-history/the-death-of-emmett-till.

hooks, bell. *Teaching To Transgress: Education as the Practice of Freedom* (New York: Routledge, 1984)

Jessica Guynn, "Facebook While Black: Users Call It Getting 'Zucked,' Say Talking about Racism Is Censored as Hate Speech," USA Today, Gannett Satellite Information Network, July 9, 2020. https://www.usatoday.com/story/news/2019/04/24/facebook-while-black-zucked-users-say-they-get-blocked-racism-discussion/2859593002/.

"Legacy Museum: From Enslavement to Mass Incarceration," Legacy Museum and National Memorial for Peace and Justice. Accessed June 9, 2021. https://museumandmemorial.eji.org/museum.

Dillon Nettles, "Foreword: Mia Raven and the P.O.W.E.R House," Foreword South, May 30, 2017. https://www.theforewordsouth.com/forewords/miaraven.

"Portrait of Mauma Mollie." WDL RSS. State Library and Archives of Florida, January 1, 1970. https://www.wdl.org/en/item/4014/.

Sumaiya Shaikh, "The Cognitive Neuroscience of a Lynching," The Wire. Accessed June 9, 2021.

https://thewire.in/science/neuroscience-lynching-autoimmune-hate.

"Social Media's Effects on Our Mental Health: All Psychology Schools," AllPsychologySchools.com, April 26, 2021.
https://www.allpsychologyschools.com/psychology/social-media-psychology/

Olivia Solon, "Facebook Ignored Racial Bias Research, Employees Say," NBCUniversal News Group, July 23, 2020. https://www.nbcnews.com/tech/tech-news/facebook-management-ignored-internal-research-showing-racial-bias-current-former-n1234746.

Emilie M. Townes, *Womanist Ethics and the Cultural Production of Evil* (New York: Palgrave Macmillan, 2006).

You Better Shoot Straight: How Maxine Waters Became Trump's Public Enemy No 1, Guardian News and Media, July 7, 2018. https://www.theguardian.com/us-news/2018/jul/07/maxine-waters-trump-progressives-california-congress.

Irvin D. Yalom and Molyn Leszcz. *The Theory and Practice of Group Psychotherapy, 5th Edition* (New York: Basic Books, 2020)

Chapter Eight:

The Confused, Alarmed, and Vulnerable: Mental Health and Psychiatry
by
Randy Meyers

Mental Health Chaplains frequently intervene in patient care with skillful application of confrontation. Sometimes this confrontation is physical. Sometimes it invites deeper insight or reduces resistance. Sometimes it helps change behavior. Chaplain Randy Meyers illustrates how confrontation in inpatient mental health treatment is necessary and is often effectively a part of overall recovery.

David Augsburger, author of *Caring Enough to Confront*, is known to have said, "Creative living is care-fronting in conflict." Mental Healthcare Chaplains frequently intervene in patient care with skillful application of confrontation to show care. Confrontation is "an open, honest identification of the client's self-defeating patterns or manipulations." [1] Sometimes it invites deeper insight or reduces resistance.[2] Sometimes it helps change behavior, deepens relationships, and builds community. The context I work within is a large freestanding inpatient

Christian mental health care hospital. I work with our children and adolescents, and with adults with a co-occurring mental illness and substance use disorder. Each unit within the hospital has two chaplains and each chaplain cares for patients in three or four units.

Confrontation often occurs within mental healthcare settings in the context of boundary setting such as when a teen patient wants to touch another patient and staff remind them of the rules. Frequent confrontation might come around behavior which is inappropriate for group context or makes group processing difficult. In these settings the group facilitator can prompt for appropriate behavior, encourage the patient to take a break, or request that the patient take a break. If disruptions continue or escalate, staff are asked to assist the patient in taking a break, or staff may remove the audience by asking all the peers in the group to change location, which leaves staff to continue to assist the disruptive patient that moment.

When offering to intervene with "care-frontation" with patient needs, the chaplain in a mental healthcare context must balance the three ethical principles of autonomy, nonmaleficence, and beneficence. Each patient admitted to the hospital is deemed to be in danger of harm to self, harm to others, or is struggling to maintain activities of daily living. The chaplain navigates the tension between these three ethical principles, such as when a patient who is given full autonomy might wish to harm themselves, the chaplain must intervene in such a way as to maximize beneficence and minimize maleficence.

What follows in this chapter are three examples of patient confrontation that illustrate the practice of confrontation. While balancing these ethical considerations, chaplains within a mental health context invite patients to consider insights into their healing, to create deeper relationships, and to integrate more fully into their community. When done poorly, confrontation breaks, or challenges, community. It seems counter-intuitive then to suggest that confrontation can be an invitation to deeper relationships. Yet confrontation done well is a powerful form of community building. MacClustie shows four benefits of ethical confrontation, to promote insight and awareness, to reduce resistance, and to promote open communication, and lead to changes in behaviors, emotions and actions.[3]

Melody, Alice and Kammy

The following case of Melody, Alice, and Kammy (not their real names) illustrates the interplay between the three ethical principles and how confrontation can promote open communication and change behaviors and actions as well as restore autonomy in community. Autonomy unchecked could have led to someone getting hurt. The confrontation guided by the principle of beneficence, restored their autonomy by reducing harm to self and their relationships.

Melody was attempting to hurt Alice, and staff members were in her way. Melody was frustrated that she could not achieve her goal, so she started to hurt herself. Her autonomy was functioning in an unhealthy way and threatening the community. Other patients and staff members were in danger of being hurt. A *Code Green* was called, which meant that more staff members were needed to assist with the devolving situation. I responded to the code, and as I came onto the unit, I wondered how I could help.

I saw Melody, a physically strong, mid-teens girl held to the floor by four staff members, who were keeping her from hurting Alice. Alice was also held to the floor by four staff members, several feet away around the corner on the other side of the nurses' station. They could not see each other, but Melody was yelling loudly at Alice. Alice, a smaller and younger teenage girl, was terrified. In her fear, Alice was attempting to hurt herself.

It was then that I noticed Kammy, another larger mid-teenaged girl, walking towards the busy nurses' station. If Kammy could not help either of her peers, she was threatening to hurt staff. Kammy had three staff members trailing her trying desperately to keep her out of the fray. Staff loudly spoke in vain, "Kammy, stop, we need you to turn around." I quickly walked towards Kammy, followed by two staff members who were ready for action.

I previously had developed a playful relationship with Kammy. This playful pastoral relationship became important to my intervention with Kammy, and in this case, my confrontation in turn strengthened my relationship with her. Knapp states, "confrontation helps the counselor better understand the genuine effects of the client's history and experience, thereby contributing to the effectiveness of the therapeutic alliance." [4]

As I approached Kammy, she reached out to stiff arm me, palm out, as if to say, "talk to the hand." I instinctively reached out in a handshake gesture, and said, "Oh, you want to shake my hand? How nice!" To my surprise, she shook my hand, and said, "Hi Chaplain." I closed my fingers and kept my thumb up and loudly and dramatically asked, "Oh, so you want to play Thumb-War with me?" M.E. Young shows that, "Some clients may find the use of humor or exaggeration by the professional counselor to be less harsh or "mean" and more fun, which helps put client behaviors or discrepancies in a more positive light and allows clients to own the discrepancies." [5]

I spun around 180 degrees and started backing up, away from the nurses' station. Kammy followed me, while I loudly counted, "One, two, three, four. I declare a thumb-war!" By the time we reached the farthest part of the unit, away from the nurses' station, she had successfully beat me by pinning down my thumb to my fingers! I loudly announced to the five staff walking quietly behind her, "Line up. Who's next?" After successfully winning against all staff, Kammy asked, "Who wants to arm wrestle me?"

Fortunately, these dramatic situations are extremely rare. Typically, my chaplain interventions during crisis codes consist of supporting staff. However, in this instance, my ability to come face-to-face with Kammy and confront her in this manner, depended to a large degree on my previous empathic and playful pastoral relationship that I had built with her. It is possible that without my confrontation, Kammy may have ended up needing to be held to the floor by staff. As it turned out, my "care-frontation" of quite literally getting in Kammy's face in a playful manner, helped restore her autonomy.

More broadly, the fact that someone is in a locked inpatient unit means their autonomy has already been functioning in a harmful manner. When someone wants to seriously hurt themselves or others, mental healthcare staff are trained to intervene. In this case, if left completely autonomous, Melody would have hurt Alice, Alice would have hurt herself, and Kammy would have hurt staff. Ralph Underwood, author of *Empathy and Confrontation in Pastoral Care* shares that "confrontation, then, invites persons to extend and enrich their participation in community. Such participation in community is essential to the development of character and transformation of spirit." [6]

When I came face-to-face with Kammy, she had declared war. She wanted to escalate violence. Strong and Zeeman show how we can connect in a more meaningful way with patients through confrontation developing greater cooperation.[7] I confronted Kammy with a thumb-war to stop the violence and restore her place in the community. Staff were ready to "go hands on" and quickly pivoted when it became clear they could engage in healthy touch. This ended in a literal holding of hands as staff successively arm-wrestled Kammy. It was not surprising that after each staff had completed their thumb-war, Kammy invited us all to an arm-wrestling competition. Her autonomy was restored, and she was empowered to extend and enrich her participation in the community. She did not need to hurt staff anymore and was able to play with staff. Similarly, by this point, Alice had also calmed down and was working with her nurse to wrap her injuries and process how she could come to staff and ask for help. Melody had also calmed down and was in her room processing with her staff the grief which had triggered her initial outburst.

Lil Wayne

In the next example, the confrontation I had with Wayne, a.k.a. Lil Wayne (not his real name) challenged deeper insight about himself, a new understanding of his behavior, and an invitation or avenue to build deeper relationships. Lil Wayne was a white male, mid-forties, and highly religious Christian who approached me after I led a short fifteen-minute Morning Reflection on one of our hospital's co-occurring disorders units. Lil Wayne had been boisterous and gregarious in the group and seemed to be hypomanic. Several African American patients had affectionately called him Lil Wayne, a moniker he may have given himself. He seemed to be trying hard to live up to this persona. Lil Wayne seemed a caricature of someone living larger than life; and at the same time, I could tell it was not going so well for him at this moment. After the Morning Reflection, other patients left the room while Lil Wayne hung back, expectantly shook my hand, and eagerly asked if I had time to talk.

Confrontation is often useful when working with patients with co-occurring mental illness and substance use disorders. "Building rapport with people who misuse substances is sometimes difficult because support, caring, and empathy have to be combined with a straightforward and realistic approach that may involve confrontation, persuasion, monitoring, and limit setting." [8] I will show a sampling of the dialogue I had with Lil Wayne, not just talk about the case, in order to illustrate how empathic listening confronts someone with what they are saying and with what they are not saying. It challenges them to face themselves.

On the surface, Lil Wayne seemed to be connecting with everyone around him; yet, as I listened, I came to see that due to his mental illness he wasn't seeing how his behavior was damaging his most intimate community, the community that is his marriage. In order for confrontation to promote insight, it needs to be done in an empowering way. Poor confrontation squashes peoples' power and wages a frontal assault on their autonomy. Confrontation done well promotes insight and honors the patient's autonomy. Lil Wayne had a superficial self-understanding and, whether he was placed on a pedestal or was placing himself on a pedestal, he struggled to see how he could enrich his participation in community.[9] Empathic confrontation can help patients to understand discrepancies and contradictions between their words and actions[10] by creating a dissonance that can serve as motivation for them to resolve. Lil Wayne was struggling with deep shame around his mental illness and substance use disorder. He had internalized a moral sense that he would not pay attention and that he would not stop drinking. His wife was reinforcing this shame. I empathically challenged his shame by reflecting back to him a deeper understanding that he could not manage these aspects of his life. This experience of my radical acceptance of his limitations forced Lil Wayne to evaluate his distorted understanding, consider a healthier narrative, and provided an opportunity to change his maladaptive beliefs.

The challenge began as Lil Wayne wanted to talk to me in the community space. I invited him to a quieter consultation room, hoping he could calm down in a smaller space with a smaller audience. As we walked to a consultation room, he asked me what I thought was the definition of grace. I told him I wanted to learn more about him and his question. He had a written journal with him that he flipped through. It was filled with large scrawling phrases on each page. When we got to the consultation room he sat down and quickly wrote in his journal "Pure Grace!"

From the outset it seemed acceptance was what Lil Wayne was looking for. As he shared his story, it became clear that he was looking to experience grace himself. He was also longing to experience grace from his wife. She recently separated from him and he did not like it. He was afraid of divorce because it went against his religious belief. He wanted to get back together and to thrive in their marriage. He loved his wife and yet did not see how he was damaging their relationship. Below is an excerpt of the conversation.

> Wayne1: "My whole life it seems like I have been looking for grace. It can be exhausting."
>
> Randy 1: "You've been searching for grace for a long time. That sounds exhausting."
>
> W2: "It is. I just can't seem to find it."
>
> R2: "Please help me understand. You just can't seem to find grace."
>
> W3: "My wife keeps telling me she wants me to give her grace. She says that I should accept what is,

without trying to control everything. She wants me to slow down and to be more present for her. Me? I like to go; to get things done. I need to keep moving. I'm an executive in my company. There's a lot going on and I love what I do. But I haven't slept more than a couple hours a night in the last several weeks. (He kind of counts out to three on one hand and out to three on the other hand). And that's not good. I'm so tired, I can't sleep. It's part of why I'm here. It's not usually this bad, it has gotten worse recently. I'm not sleeping. I cannot turn off my mind. It has gotten really scary with what all I was thinking about doing. I knew I needed to come here."

R3: "I'm glad you are here. I see why you feel exhausted. It sounds like you can't slow down. You have to keep on moving. You typically have lots of energy which has served you well. But for some reason, recently it has gotten difficult to slow down mentally and to be emotionally present for your wife. Now, you are so tired you can't sleep. All this seems to have gotten in the way of your relationship and makes it harder to give grace and to experience grace."

W4: "You got it! That's me. (laughs), and here I am (gestures around to the co-occurring unit outside the consultation room) and I don't even drink that much."

R4: "You do not drink that much."

W5: "Yeah. I mean, sometimes I drink. With everything going on, a few drinks help my brain relax. It's nice to not have to think about everything."

R5: "So, it sounds like drinking helps you manage some of your emotional pain. It sounds like a kind of grace."

W6: "Not pure grace though. She doesn't like it at all."

R6: "So, it kind of helps temporarily and kind of adds to the problem with your wife."

W7: "Yep. So that's why I'm looking for grace."

R7: "I can see now why you are looking for grace for yourself. And at the same time your wife is looking for a pure gift from you too. However, Wayne, it seems like the very grace she wants from you is something that is very difficult for you to give her. And right now, right now, it feels impossible to give her."

W8: "Now that I'm reflecting on this with you, I've never really thought of it this way before."

R8: "What has this dynamic been like for you?"

W9: "It is frustrating."

R9: "It sounds very frustrating."

W10: "It's not like I'm a bad person or anything. I love her more than anything; that's part of why I work so much, and also why I'm here."

R10: "I hear how much you love her. You don't see yourself as a bad person."

W11: "It's just so embarrassing. She keeps asking me to give more of myself and I just can't do it. I feel so bad about this."

R11: "You feel embarrassed by what you can't give her. (Pause) Earlier, you told me about the strengths of your quick thinking; how your brain has served you well in life and in your business. In many areas, it's been such an asset. It sounds like you've tried to show your wife this. And she asks you for this whole other thing that's on the complete other side of your strength; the side you can't give to her right now."

W12: "Yep exactly! I feel ashamed, I give so much, and I can't do this for her."

R12: "So it's not that you won't give her grace, it is that you can't, and maybe can't is too strong, here, and yet it is very difficult though."

W13: "Exactly. (Sighs. Pauses to write in journal). I'm going to reflect more on "won't" and "can't."

R13: "As I've listened to you, I hear you finding grace for yourself by reflecting on your limitations."

W14: (laughs) "My wife needs to accept them."

R14: "Well, if she were here, I could listen to her. (He laughs.) And you are the one who is here working hard on finding grace for yourself. I see you starting to accept the limitations of the way you think and the way that impacts your relationship with your wife."

W15: "True. (pauses) I am hopeful though (pointing at the doctor's chair in the consultation room). I just need some help to sleep and clear my thinking. We're trying some medication the doctor thinks will provide relief for my anxiety and depression. So, we'll see how that goes."

R15: "You seem hopeful that medication might be a kind of grace to you and your wife."

W16: (He sits silently, begins to write slowly in his journal.) "As I'm telling it to you now, I haven't thought of it quite this way before. I knew medicine wasn't magic or anything. It might be part of the picture, like with these groups and all the coping stuff here, but medication might be able to give me something that I don't have. (He pauses to write.) Ok, wow. Thank you so much for listening to me."

R16: "You are welcome."

This interaction with Wayne illustrates how empathic confrontation can help a patient come to new insight through challenging his understanding that he would not give grace to his wife. Initially, I highly doubted Wayne was asking me for an actual textbook theological definition about the concept of grace. What Wayne wanted was to experience grace. On one level he wanted grace from his wife, though he was phrasing it as she wanted grace from him. On another, I perceived he needed to experience grace for his own limitations, so I sought to embody grace to him.

In the narrative, from W4-R5 I confront his alcohol use by naming it as a grace, which challenged him to deeper honesty in W6. In R6 I name that as maladaptive for his relationship. This confrontation allowed him to face the consequences of his alcohol and its impact was worse, at least according to his wife, than he first let on.

In R7 I challenge this understanding of what is in his control and what is not easily under his control. He responds with a deeper expression of his emotions, frustration, embarrassment, and shame. In my embodiment of grace to him, Wayne begins to imagine confronting his wife (W14). However, I use humor (R14) to challenge him to keep the focus on himself and his impact on his wife. In W15 and W16 Wayne starts to name a grace, in the form of medication, and accept that grace, for himself.

My coming face-to-face with Wayne allowed him to see something new in his relationship and within himself. Indeed, it can be irritating to have someone asking you for grace in a graceless manner, demanding from you something that you cannot give. Wayne tries so hard to be graceful with others but struggles to accept his limitations or his difficult emotions about those limitations. While the focus is on Wayne, his wife may also benefit from acceptance of his limitations, but his health needs to start with himself, and probably his drinking behavior.

Eric and Sam

The case of Wayne illustrated subtle and supportive empathic confrontation. There are other more direct examples of confrontation in mental health care. Before each group, chaplains will go around the unit to let people know that the groups will begin shortly. These brief encounters offer invitations to attend, clarify any concerns patients might have about the nature or content of the group, and since group work is essential to patient healing, chaplains challenge patients to engage in their own healing work. These very brief interactions with patients can at times be confrontational. These confrontations can reduce resistance or open up communication. Gadgila notes that people who are forced to compare their flawed perceptions with a more realistic understanding, can begin a process of positive change of their beliefs and ideas.[11]

For example, after sharing with patients in the milieu that Morning Reflection will begin shortly in the quiet lounge, I will often receive comments like, "Wait, is it religious?" Sometimes I offer a playful, yet confrontational, response. "Oh, no, I'm sorry it is not. Why is that something you were looking for?" From there the patient either laughs or chokes out somewhat disgustedly, "No. I don't do religious groups." I then engage more empathically, "Oh. It sounds like you have had a prior bad experience with other religious people or a judgmental religious group." This reflection serves to set a clarifying boundary.

A helpful process for evaluating a patient's response is the five-point Client Change Scale (CCS). The CCS stages are denial, partial examination, full examination but no change, decides to live with incongruity, and decides to change from incongruity. The confrontation clarifies whether or not the patient is simply misinformed, is inconsistent, or is in conflict. When chaplains "listen and question in particular ways that help clients expose and evaluate perspectives and practices the client has taken for granted and that draw out, identify, and amplify clients' preferred directions, their strengths, and exceptions to problems."[12] MacCluskie notes that confrontation is "making an observation or otherwise bringing to a client's attention discrepancies that are apparent to the counselor in the client's behavior, feelings, or perception."[13] There are a number of discrepancies that chaplains can listen for.[14] Six types of discrepancies exist between verbal and nonverbal messages, beliefs and experiences, values and behavior, talk and behavior, experiences and plans, and verbal messages. Strong and Zeman show how confrontation can help chaplains connect more deeply with the patients, directing patients to specific work, or improving the therapeutic alliance by working together.[15] Knapp says that confrontation helps patients "identify and process discrepancies that may resolve with clarification."[16]

The following case of Eric illustrates a much more direct style of confrontation. It partially illustrates a cautionary tale of how not to confront. It also illustrates patient autonomy as Eric scores lower on the Client Change Scale than Sam.

The story also illustrates how, when a patient like Sam is ready to work, an empathic challenge can be just the confrontation they need to experience significant spiritual growth.

Eric, a white male in his early 20's with borderline personality disorder, had sworn at admission staff when they screened him for religious or spiritual care needs. He did not "bleeping" want a visit from a Chaplain. When I walked onto the unit to lead my wellness group Eric loudly announced to peers and staff that he would not be attending a wellness group. He seemed to be joking around with his peers that he was playing cards with so I playfully inquired, "Oh? Why is that?" He explained that he was not into wellness groups. Again, I tried to playfully challenge him to greater clarity by asking, "If it was an illness group, would you be into that?" This challenge which had worked so well on the co-occurring disorders unit, did not work so well with this young adult on our young adult unit. I could tell from his loud angry response that he was not coming to the group. In retrospect, had I known at the time about his past religiously traumatic history and his current diagnosis of borderline personality disorder, I would not have challenged him so directly.

I continued to the other patients to attend—most patients left him behind and came to the group. However, during the group time Eric curled up on the floor in a fetal position and worked himself up into a panic attack. Through loud dramatic tears, he told staff they should prohibit me from coming on to the unit. He explained he had been abused by a religious leader in his past and seeing a chaplain, any chaplain, was a trigger. After the group, multiple staff, including his nurse, doctor, an activity therapist, and his case manager individually came to my office to tell me of Eric's request. They had picked up his anxiety and were sharing his concern with me.

I calmly and directly explained to staff that to my knowledge I was not the religious figure who hurt him. I had training to not hurt him. He was in a safe place to explore his trauma, if he would like to. Other patients had the right to receive spiritual care from a chaplain. Staff were supportive and realized that his dramatic flair made this particular situation complicated. I asked them to remind him that just as he could choose to attend any group or choose to not attend any group, they would support him with his needs whether he attended or not. I also spoke with his psychiatrist who could see that I represented an opportunity for him to challenge his beliefs and assumptions. His case manager suggested to him a model of gradual exposure given the severity of his reaction. I did not go looking for Eric, and in the end, he managed to avoid me and my group for the rest of this admission, so we did not process this incident.

However, about a month after his discharge, Eric was readmitted. Once again, in the process of inviting all the patients on the unit, I invited Eric and the peers he was playing cards with to the group. I had made this decision to invite him to the group, because I did not want to assume that he had not changed. Eric once again loudly complained to his peers about my presence, they laughed, and while Eric did not join my group, to my surprise, several peers joined the group. I let Eric know that if he changed his mind, he was welcome to attend this wellness group which was not a religious group.

One peer who joined was Sam, another early 20's white male who had depression and an anxiety disorder. Later, after the group, Sam admitted to me that he had only come to the group to challenge me. Yet seeing how I had respected everyone in the group, he was unable to poke fun of me. Near the end of the group, Sam asked for an individual consultation. During the consultation, he shared that he had a similar negative experience with a past religious leader as did Eric. Yet seeing the boundaries I set with Eric before the group, and experiencing the boundaries Sam experienced in the group, helped Sam come to see that he could change his own behavior, engage productively in treatment, and explore a spiritually and religiously conflicted part of himself.

On his day of discharge, Sam asked his staff to call me back to the unit because he wanted to thank me for the important role I played in challenging him to his own healing work, and to celebrate his personal and spiritual growth. This situation with Eric and Sam may be on the more extreme side of the confrontation spectrum, yet there are lessons to learn. Particularly that confrontation is best delivered empathically, sincerely, and playfully, not to mention offered sensitively and pastorally.

However, not every patient will respond to every intervention with the same level of change. For example, chaplains may need different boundaries with pre-contemplative patients than with patients managing their change well.

Summary

To care well, mental healthcare chaplains must confront well because patients will not care how much you know unless they know deep down that you care about them and their needs. At times, chaplains intervene by confronting patients in a dynamic process, whereby the chaplain assists patients to greater insight or awareness and can reduce resistance or open up communication. Chaplain confrontation can powerfully provide boundaries necessary for a healthy balance of autonomy, nonmaleficence, and beneficence.

Confrontation can restore, strengthen, and deepen relationships within a community. Confrontation helps some patients gain new understanding of their situation, especially when they experience an acceptance of their own conflicted inner narrative, which can positively shift their view of themselves and their situation.

When done poorly, confrontation in pastoral care can further isolate patients. It can harm or reinforce unhealthy patterns of patient behaviors, beliefs, or ideas. However, when conflict is effectively employed by the chaplain, patients are more able to change harmful behaviors and maladaptive actions. Chaplains must continually assess and evaluate the effectiveness of their confrontation and adapt their interventions accordingly. The successful application of empathic confrontation can assist patients live a healthier lifestyle [3,5,10,17,18] When practiced well, chaplains who intervene with confrontation can significantly assist patients find clarity and serenity and feel more secure in themselves and their own actions.

Contact Info: Randy Myers, MDiv, DMin, BCC, APC Board Certified Chaplain, Pine Rest Christian Counseling Center, Grand Rapids, MI RandyandLynae@yahoo.com

[1] David Augsburger, *Caring Enough to Confront: How to understand and express your deepest feelings toward others*, 3rd Edition (Grand Rapids, Revell, 2009).

[2] Leaman, DR, "Confrontation in Counseling," *Personnel & Guidance Journal;* v. 56 (10), (1978), 630-633.

[3] Kathryn MacCluskie, *Acquiring Counseling Skills: Integrating Theory, Multiculturalism, and Self-Awareness* (Hoboken: Prentice Hall, 2010).

[4] Herschel Knapp, *Therapeutic communication: Developing professional skills* (Thousand Oaks: Sage Publications, 2007)

[5] Mark E. Young, *Learning the art of helping: Building blocks and techniques,* (New York: Pearson, 2013)

[6] Ralph Underwood, *Empathy and Confrontation in Pastoral Care* (Eugene: Wipf and Stock, 2002), 92.

[7] Strong, T, & Zeman, D, "Dialogic Considerations of Confrontation as a Counseling Activity: An Examination of Allen Ivey's Use of Confronting as a Microskill," *Journal of Counseling & Development*, v. 88, (2010), 332-339.

[8] Lourie W. Reichenberg and Linda Seligman, *Selecting Effective Treatments: A Comprehensive, Systematic Guide to Treating Mental Disorders,* third edition (Hoboken: John Wiley & Sons, 2007), 303

[9] Underwood, ibid.

[10] Allen E Ivey, Mary B. Ivey, Carlos P Zalaquett, *Essentials of intentional interviewing* (Belmont: Brooks/Cole, 2012).

[11] Gadgila, S, Nokes-Malacha, TJ, and Chib, MT. "Effectiveness of Holistic Mental Model Confrontation in Driving Conceptual Change," *Learning and Instruction,* v. 22(1), (2010), 47-61, doi:10.1016/j.learninstruc.2011.06.002

[12] KA Fall, JM Holden and A Marquis, *Theoretical Models of Counseling and Psychotherapy* (New York: Routledge, 2010), 362

[13] Kathryn MacCluskie, *Acquiring counseling skills: Integrating theory, multiculturalism, and self-awareness,* (NJ: Pearson/Merrill, 2010), 162.

[14] Ivey, AE, & Daniels, T, "Systematic Interviewing Microskills and Neuroscience: Developing Bridges between the Fields of Communication and Counseling Psychology,". *International Journal of Listening,* (2016), 30, 3, 99-119.15

[15] Strong, ibid.

[16] Gottlieb, MC, Handelsman, MM, & Knapp, S, "Some principles for ethics education: Implementing the acculturation model," *Training and Education in Professional Psychology*, (2008), 2(3), 139.

[17] Shechtman, Z and Yanov, H, "Interpretives (confrontation, interpretation, and feedback) in preadolescent counseling groups,". *Group Dynamics: Theory, Research, and Practice*, (2001) 5(2), 124–135. https://doi.org/10.1037/1089-2699.5.2.124

[18] Gerald Corey, *Theory and Practice of Group Counseling*, 10th ed. (Boston: Cengage Learning, 2013).

Chapter Nine:

The Core-Shaken: Confronting Moral Injury with Combat Veterans in Groups
by
Chaplain Gregory J Widmer

Combat veteran and clinical supervision Gregory Widmer knows by his own experience how deep are buried the devastating experiences of seeing, hearing, remembering and acting out feelings about people killing and being killed by one another. He has subsequently learned through relatively successful treatment programs how to assist as a V.A. chaplain, the recovery process that is so difficult and shows such unpredictable success. What he has learned about confrontation of recovering combat veterans may teach us something more about this intricate intervention.

War is nothing new to the human experience. The oldest annals of history record combat. What is newer, at least from a Western perspective, is the understanding of just how devastating guilt and shame that follows combat can be. These feelings of guilt and shame frequently lead to what is broadly categorized as *moral injury*. While most chaplains are familiar with post-traumatic stress disorder (PTSD), fewer understand moral injury, and fewer still know how to assist in treating it.

Chaplains are uniquely positioned to participate in the process of moral reintegration. Chaplains are clinically necessary given the holistic impact of moral injury. Spirituality/religion has been shown to (A) mitigate moral injury; or (B) exacerbate moral injury; or (C) be affected by moral injury.[1] Responding to it is within the chaplain's role and indeed a necessary component of that role.

In other words, moral injury is a wounding of the soul. Research has suggested that PTSD and moral injury in combination are a risk factor for suicide attempts.[2] The stakes could not be any higher.

This chapter has three goals.

1. Define moral injury vis-à-vis PTSD.

2. Describe moral reintegration using Acceptance and Commitment Therapy (ACT).

3. Demonstrate the benefits of confrontation in veterans who participated in a moral injury group.

Define Moral Injury

In order to understand moral injury, let's begin by looking at several definitions. One of the most commonly cited definitions of moral injury is it is harm caused by: Perpetrating, failing to prevent, witnessing, or learning about actions that violate deeply held moral beliefs and expectations…thus, the key precondition for moral injury is an act of transgression, which shatters moral and ethical expectations that are rooted in religious or spiritual beliefs, or culture-based, organizational, and group-based rules about fairness, the value of life, and so forth.[3]

Other definitions include:[4]

• The existential, psychological, emotional, and or spiritual trauma arising from a conflict, violation or betrayal, either by omission or commission, of or within one's moral beliefs or code(s).[5]

• Phenomenologically, moral injury represents a particular trauma syndrome including psychological, existential, behavioral and interpersonal issues that emerge following perceived violations of deep moral beliefs by 1. oneself, or, 2. trusted individuals (i.e., morally injurious experiences). These experiences cause significant moral dissonance, which if unresolved leads to the development of core and secondary symptoms.[6]

• Changes in biological, psychological, social, or spiritual functioning resulting from witnessing or perpetrating acts, or failures to act, that transgress deeply held, communally shared moral beliefs and expectations.[7]

As is highlighted above, moral injury is identified and assessed in numerous ways, but at its core is distinguished by whether intrusive thoughts are rooted in fear (PTSD) or *rooted in guilt, shame, anger and betrayal* (moral injury).

For example, being in a firefight produces understandable fear and thus may lead to PTSD. After the fighting is over, however, witnessing the aftermath may be equally or more distressing. In this scenario, PTSD and moral injury occur from the same engagement, but their roots are different. The following visual highlights the core differences.

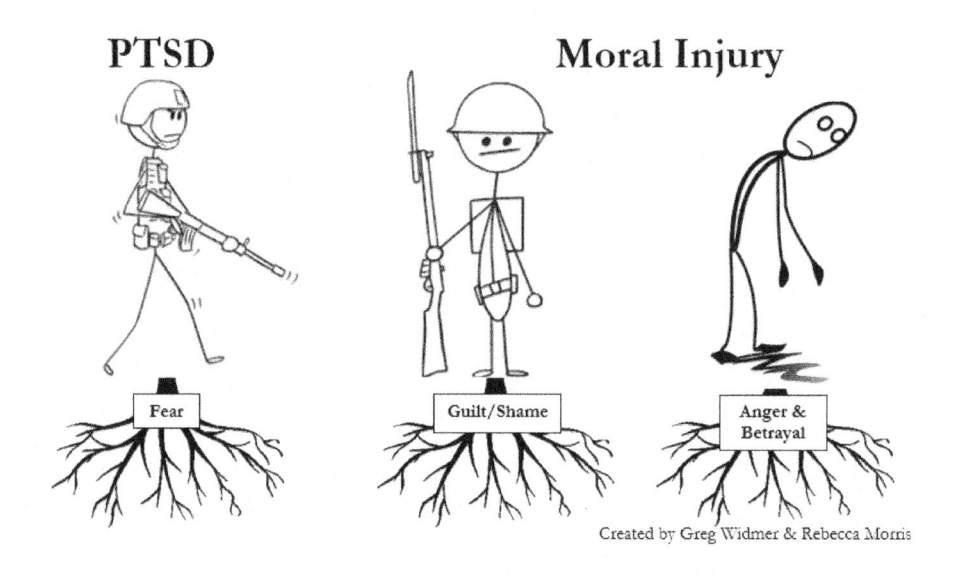

PTSD — Fear

Moral Injury — Guilt/Shame — Anger & Betrayal

Created by Greg Widmer & Rebecca Morris

To get even more technical, not all moral offenses cause moral injury. To be sure, moral offenses cause moral pain, but *it is only the avoidance of that pain that leads to moral injury* (i.e., suffering). For example, to witness innocent civilians impacted by war is a moral offense (civilians should not be causalities of war) that produces moral pain (it is painful to watch innocent civilians suffer). The difference with whether or not a moral offense leads to moral injury is how the subject copes with it.

In this scenario, Veteran A who sees the suffering of innocent civilians may feel the pain, and yet deal with it in a healthy way (e.g., engage in therapy, positive emotional coping, discuss the event with trusted allies). However, another veteran, Veteran B, who witnesses the same event may engage in avoidance strategies like excessive drinking, workaholism, or interpersonal conflict. Both Veterans A and B witnessed a moral offense and both experienced moral pain. But only Veteran B suffers from moral injury due to the avoidance of this moral pain. In other words, *how a person responds to a moral offense or handles their moral pain will determine whether or not they experience a moral injury.*

The following graphic shows the progression of moral injury from beginning to end.

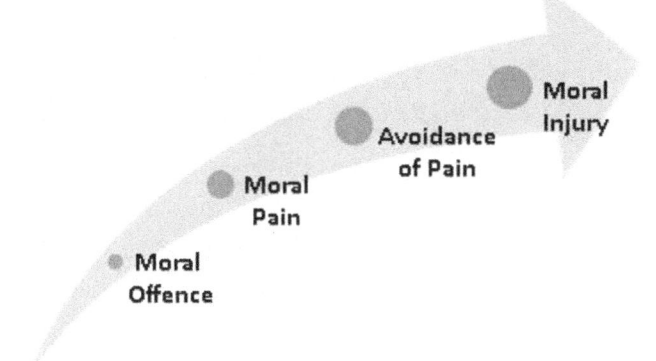

Describing Moral Reintegration

It is necessary for clinical chaplains to know about moral injury. They are likely to meet it in many combat veterans hospitalized for a variety of reasons every day. Morality is often complexly intertwined with issues of religion, faith, and spirituality for many individuals.[8] Another reason is that moral injury may erode their sense of meaning and place in the world, even challenging their faith.[9] This loss of meaning in life has been linked to suicidal ideation.[10] Yet knowledge alone is not sufficient; experiential learning in community also needs to be present to address moral injury. The reason community is important is because *moral injury occurs in community and thus heals in community.*

Moral reintegration follows the opposite trajectory of moral injury wherein an individual accepts their pain and sees that there was a value violated by the moral offense. The last step is to live a life committed to that value(s) which is the hallmark of moral reintegration.

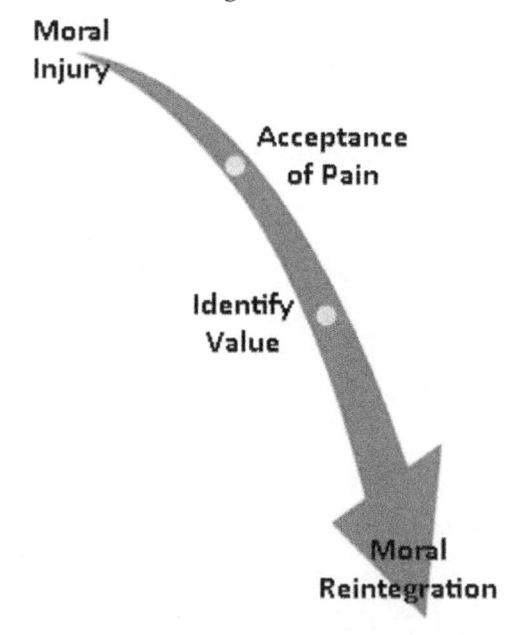

Moral Injury → Acceptance of Pain → Identify Value → Moral Reintegration

In the Department of Veterans Affairs, a pioneering moral injury group was started by psychologist Dr. Jaimie Lusk (Salem, Oregon Vet Center) and Chaplain Rebecca Morris (Portland VA Health Care System). Their pioneering work has proven beneficial for many Veterans, including for this writer. After going through the program as a participant, this writer has had the opportunity to teach the group numerous times. The group is called ACT for Moral Injury wherein "ACT" stands for "Acceptance and Commitment Therapy."

ACT for Moral Injury fits into the broader framework of Chaplain Service known collectively as "Progressions Program."

Progressions Program is based on Dr. Judith Herman's three-stage model of recovery.[11] In her 1997 book, *Trauma and Recovery*, she describes in detail the healing process of people who struggle with a combination of problems related to unwanted, abusive, or traumatic experiences. The Portland VA Health Care System's Chaplain Service has modified those processes into three phases of healing:

Phase 1: Stabilization
Phase 2: Trauma-Processing
Phase 3: Reintegration

ACT for Moral Injury is a Phase 2.5 group that comes *post trauma-processing*. What that means is that a veteran needs to have done an evidence-based psychotherapy (EBP) such as cognitive processing theory (CPT) or prolonged exposure (PE) before engaging in ACT for Moral Injury.

The following chart is an overview of the 10-week group. Take note of the integration of mental health and spirituality, which is a cornerstone of the group. In fact, the group is co-facilitated by a chaplain and a mental health provider.

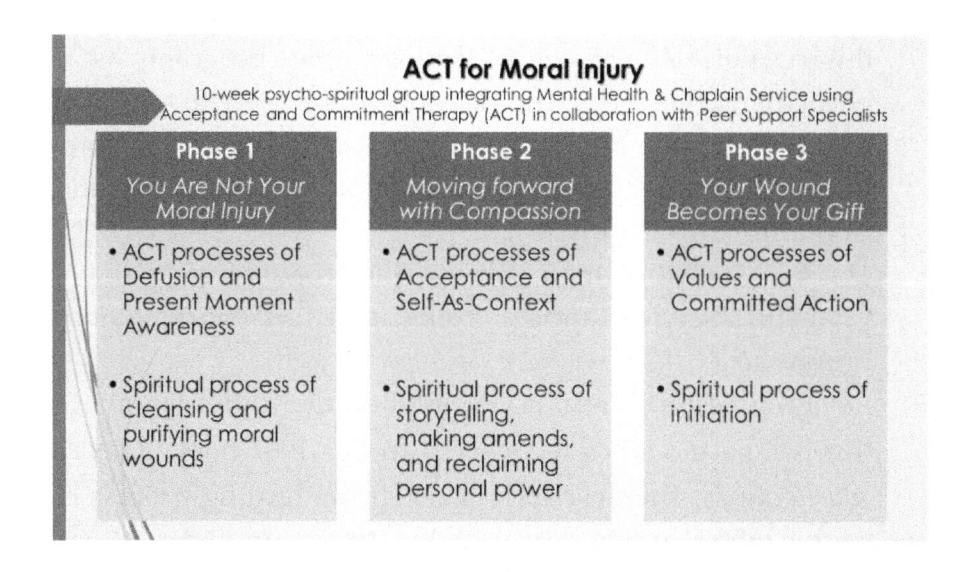

ACT for Moral Injury

10-week psycho-spiritual group integrating Mental Health & Chaplain Service using Acceptance and Commitment Therapy (ACT) in collaboration with Peer Support Specialists

Phase 1	Phase 2	Phase 3
You Are Not Your Moral Injury	*Moving forward with Compassion*	*Your Wound Becomes Your Gift*
• ACT processes of Defusion and Present Moment Awareness	• ACT processes of Acceptance and Self-As-Context	• ACT processes of Values and Committed Action
• Spiritual process of cleansing and purifying moral wounds	• Spiritual process of storytelling, making amends, and reclaiming personal power	• Spiritual process of initiation

Now that we have an understanding of what moral injury is and a brief overview of the ten-week group, we will now turn our attention to examples of veterans who participated in this group and what their experience was like.

Confrontation of In-Treatment Combat Veterans with Moral Injury

Confrontation through Symbols

In the ACT for Moral Injury group, veterans are confronted silently through the use of symbols. At the beginning of a group, veterans are asked to bring an object that symbolizes their moral injury. Some veterans eagerly accept this assignment while others bristle or conceive of this as chaplain woo-woo. Nevertheless, each week they are invited to place that object on an altar and thereby externalize their wound symbolically. Throughout the ten weeks, their moral injury object sits in front of them on the altar and serves as a symbol for why they are there.

Another symbol used is a two-sided rock. Underneath each moral injury there is a broken value. In order to symbolize this, veterans take a rock and on one side write their moral injury in one word, while on the other side they write the value that was violated. This tends to be a time of enlightenment for many veterans because they realize that the reason moral injury hurts so much is because it violated a core value. Values such as family, meaning, freedom, and love are often written on one side while the moral injuries of combat, military sexual trauma, casualties, and erosion of truth are written on the flip side.

Yet another symbol that confronts veterans is a symbol that represents their committed action. While there are other symbols in the group, these three (moral injury symbol, two-sided rock, and committed action symbol) highlight the healing properties of symbols.

Much like sacramental theology, these ordinary objects are catalysts for unseen transformation. One Operation Iraqi Freedom Veteran remarked, "The two-sided rock and the ceremony of intentionally placing a moral injury item on the altar, helped me to get space from the moral injury."

Confrontation through Provocation

A primary reason that ACT for Moral Injury has been so successful is due to its co-creator, Chaplain Rebecca Morris. She has an uncanny ability to lean into tension and help draw out the heart of combat veterans. Her style of chaplaincy is affectionately known as 'coyote medicine' based on the years of training she has had with tribal peoples.

One Marine remarked that, "It was the coyote medicine constantly challenging me to make a statement, call out my emotional content, 'say it from your heart RIGHT NOW,' without time for me to intellectualize my response. I disliked this because it meant I could not filter my own reaction through the stories I told myself, and what I believed I was (a monster). It was where I began to encounter my authentic truth and challenged my beliefs for my benefit."

Another veteran stated that, "I also greatly appreciated how the facilitators tactfully pushed against my resistances in order to expose the areas I most needed to work on, and by doing so taught me that I was much more capable of addressing the most painful parts of my moral injury than I had thought possible."

Combat Veterans are brave individuals. They can handle being confronted about their inner world. For example, this writer recalls an interaction with a Green Beret whose index trauma was a jungle ambush. During the war, this Veteran was in a leadership position and decided to take point—the most dangerous position during patrols. His team was on a patrol in the jungle when they were suddenly ambushed. The veteran was immediately hit by gunfire and fell backwards. And with tears in his eyes he recounts, "And I lost some of my guys." It was obvious to this writer that as tragic as the situation was, he had nothing to be ashamed about. He led from the front, literally, and displayed true valor in combat. And yet he remained haunted that some soldiers died on his watch. This writer gently brought this to his attention saying, "You were so brave leading from the front; it's not your fault that they died." His response highlights the challenge of moral reintegration and that it takes time to heal these wounds. "Yeah, that might be, but they were still my guys." In this case, the veteran has yet to see his huge heart behind this tragic loss.

Confrontation through Community

This writer recalls a confrontation with another Marine from the Iraq War. He was suffering from PTSD and substance-use disorder, and this writer was educating him about moral injury. While he got the concept, he was clearly starting to shut down.

He finally said, "Chaplain, I can't take yet another thing wrong with me at this time." That is when it became clear that *moral injury is not what's wrong with someone, but what is right with them.* While this veteran had a hard time hearing this, subsequent veterans have found this type of confrontation—namely that moral injury reflects their goodness—extremely helpful.

> The fruit of confrontation is that veterans realize that moral injury is an indication that the heart is broken, and the human spirit is alive and well!

Caregivers might consider confronting combat veterans who are patients in a general hospital to be counterproductive, if not intimidating. Nevertheless, the guilt and shame these veterans harbor needs elucidation in order to uncover the immense charity and love beneath the moral injuries. For chaplains who are inexperienced in working with combat veterans here are a few things to keep in mind.

Spiritual Care for Combat Veterans as Patients in a General Hospital

Chaplains may first encounter patients hospitalized for any reason who also have combat experience and untreated moral injury. Some things for chaplains to remember are:

- "Combat" veterans have different definitions of what it means to be in combat. For some, it means you have to have fired your weapon. For others, it means being deployed to a theater of war. Allow the veteran to determine whether or not they view themselves as a combat veteran.

- Follow the lead of the veteran with whether or not they want to talk about their combat experience. It may take time to build a rapport with someone before they are willing to share, if they do at all.

- Ask open-ended questions like, "How did your military experience impact you?" or "What would be helpful for me to know about your military experience?"

- Be cautious about flippantly saying, "Thank you for your service." This can be a loaded phrase. You might consider "Thank you for your sacrifice," or, "Welcome home" for Vietnam veterans, or even, "I know 'thank you for your service' can be a loaded phrase, what do you find meaningful for people to say regarding your service?" Or simply, "I deeply appreciate what you gave for our country."

- Ask them if they are enrolled in the Department of Veterans Affairs (VA) health care. Not every VA offers a moral injury group, but they are becoming increasingly more available. All a veteran need do is call their local VA and ask for eligibility/enrollment to get started.

This chapter has looked at: 1. A definition of moral injury vis-à-vis PTSD; 2. Described moral reintegration using ACT; and 3. Demonstrated the benefits of confrontation with combat veterans.

For decades to come, chaplains will need to both know about moral injury and also be able to help others reintegrate their broken values into their lives. The spiritual health of countless individuals depends on it. After all, just like PTSD is not a "veteran thing" neither is moral injury. On the contrary, moral injury impacts humans and it is this writer's hope that more and more chaplains will not only recognize it, but also use confrontation and referral to heal these partially hidden soul wounds.

Contact Info: Greg Widmer, MDiv, Chaplain and ACPE Educator Candidate, VA Hospital of Portland, OR
Gregory.Widmer@va.gov

[1] Brémault-Phillips S, Pike A, Scarcella F, Cherwick T, "Spirituality and Moral Injury Among Military Personnel: A Mini-Review," *Front Psychiatry,* 10:276, (April 29, 2019). doi: 10.3389/fpsyt.2019.00276. PMID: 31110483; PMCID:

[2] Bryan, CJ, Bryan, AO, Roberge, E, Leifker, FR, Rozek, DC, "Moral injury, posttraumatic stress disorder, and suicidal behavior among National Guard personnel," *Psychol Trauma,* 10(1), (January 2018), 36-45. doi: 10.1037/tra0000290. Epub: Jun 5, 2017. PMID: 28581315.

[3] Litz et al., 2009. "Moral injury and moral repair in war veterans: A preliminary model and intervention strategy." *Clinical Psychology Review,* 29, (2009), 695-706.

[4] A helpful article that consolidates 17 definitions of moral injury into one article: Hodgson, T and Carey, L, "Moral injury and definitional clarity: betrayal, spirituality and the role of chaplains." *Journal of Religious Health,* 56 (2017), 1212-1228.

[5] Jamieson, N, Maple, M, Ratnarajah, D, Usher, K, "Military moral injury: A concept analysis," *International Journal of Mental Health Nursing* (December 29, 2020), (6):1049-1066. doi: 10.1111/inm.12792. Epub Oct 19, 2020. PMID: 33078522.

[6] Jinkerson, JD. "Defining and assessing moral injury: A syndrome perspective," *Traumatology,* 22(2), (2016), 122-130.

[7] Nash, WP, et al, "Consensus recommendations for common data elements for operational stress research and surveillance: Report of a federal interagency working group," *Archives of Physical Medicine and Rehabilitation* 91(11), (2010), 1673-1683.

[8] Meador KG, Nieuwsma JA, "Moral Injury: Contextualized Care," *Journal of Medical Humanities,* 39(1) (March 2018), 93-99. doi: 10.1007/s10912-017-9480-2. PMID: 29027618.

[9] Jones E, "Moral injury in a context of trauma," *British Journal of Psychiatry* 216(3) (March 2020), 127-128. doi: 10.1192/bjp.2020.46. PMID: 32345414.

[10] ML Kelley, et al, "Own soul's warning: Moral injury, suicidal ideation, and meaning in life," National Institute of Health, (Oct 2021), DOI: 10.1037/tra0001047.

[11] Judith Herman, *Trauma and Recovery,* (New York: Basic Books, 1997).

Chapter Ten:

Confrontation When Words Fail
by
Joel C Graves

When scientists, psychologists and others seek to bring some clarity to the jumble of motivating sensations we call human emotions, they often name five or six basic feelings that are universal across all cultures. The most fundamental one however, is often omitted. The painful sensation of raw hurt lies beneath anger which it always underlies; is what fear is trying to avoid more of; forms the basis of sadness from something previously painfully lost; constitutes the ache of regret in guilt and shame; and can eventually be overshadowed by the only positive emotion, joy or being glad. Hurt hides. Few of us recognize it clearly even in ourselves. When it is clearly and surely recognized by another person, even non-verbally, a connection is made like no other.

In the following two stories, chaplains illustrate, though not intentionally, the "use of self" touted in certification of clinical educator formation. Both situations embody a fact that is not usually mentioned—the ways in which often, maybe always, deep hurt underlies anger, even violent rage.

In the first situation, the male chaplain intuitively and quickly responds to the hurt lurking beneath violence in the emergency department (ER) by using his own personal history semi-consciously to care in a unique way in a very difficult situation. There is a complex issue about violence in the Emergency Department, that should not be minimized. But spiritual care can happen unexpectedly as a single incident of care being needed and a chaplain being there.

When I was a resident CPE student at Saint Joseph Medical Center in Tacoma, Washington—in my third unit, the students took turns as the overnight emergency room chaplain. At one in the morning, the ambulance brought in a young man, early twenties, who had been shot three times at close range while sitting in his car by a rival gang member with a .45 caliber pistol. Over the next hour, twenty-plus Samoan gang members and relatives converged on the hospital. The staff became noticeably alarmed. The ER staff whispered speculations about whether some of the family and gang members might be armed. Tacoma police officers appeared and disappeared, taking statements from witnesses. Two surgeons labored over the young man for hours, and we could feel the tension rising. I would walk back to the operating theater, look in, then report to the family.

At four in the morning, the surgeons called the ER and told them they could not save the young man. Someone told the waiting family and all hell broke loose. The younger brother ran down the hallways smashing his fist into every glass picture hanging from the walls. ER called a Code.

I was working my way back from the operating room and saw the young man smashing pictures, surrounded by gang members. They were all very upset and looked scary. As they approached me, I blocked their progress. The younger brother had tears in his eyes and shook with grief. Blood dripped from his fists.

The only thing I can tell you is that my heart went out to him. I reached, taking his bloody hands in mine, and said, "I am so, so sorry." He let me hold his hands. At first, he stared at the floor, then he looked at me, tears flowing.

"I am so sorry your brother died," I repeated. "I can tell that you loved him deeply and it is tearing you apart—all of you."

Now, the young man leaned toward me, his head on my shoulder, and wept loudly, moaning and sobbing. This action gave permission to the other gang members to join him in their sorrow and we all wept openly. The hospital police officers arrived and slowly backed off. Another on-duty chaplain arrived with the Code and watched what was happening.

They were crying, I was crying, and after about ten minutes, we were wrung out. We walked slowly back to the ER waiting room, where his mother and father and other relatives were waiting. They all hugged each other and cried more, but the threat of violence had vanished. An hour later, they left for home.

As chaplains, we are always learning and studying how to speak to people in various settings, hoping to say the right thing at the right time and provide something useful to people in a time of crisis or pain or suffering. We learn to tease out emotions and analyze feelings, helping the person find a path, as a way to bring comfort and meaning to people.

But there comes a time when words fail us, and in some cases that can be good and necessary. The only thing left is to directly enter the suffering person's world and try to bring comfort and solace.

The next day the chaplain who witnessed the incident asked me how I knew to do that. At first, I did not understand the question. He said, "What made you take the young man's bloody hands? I would have never done that." An answer didn't jump out at me, and he thought it was a learned response, something I might have picked up in CPE training.

As I reflected on the incident, I thought my experience as a combat veteran might have informed my actions. On one level, I was not intimidated by the sight of dripping blood or violent behavior or threatening postures. Those things seemed trivial compared to the young man's palpable suffering.

When I was young, my younger brother died of leukemia. I did not realize until many, many years later, that I carried around a profound wound from that loss—a wound that never healed completely. In some respects, that also might have caused my heart to go out to this young brother. Whatever the reason, it was exactly what he needed at the time—what the whole gang and family needed. Perhaps, what I needed also.

Henri Nouwen is one of my favorite authors. He speaks of the wounded healer and how our wounded lives help us enter into the pain of others.[1] I suspect that something like that was at work. I often considered myself one of the walking wounded, because my life experiences—spiritual, mental and physical wounds—informed my chaplaincy.

Some might say, in this incident, confrontation did not happen. But I would say it is a type of confrontation, where words were not welcomed, only action, and a type of action that confronted the rage directly and then intimately.

Confrontation in situations like this can become a profound spiritual experience. In our sorrow, we were joined in the Devine—sheltered, comforted, strengthened. Before, in our anger and suffering, we were in the darkness of despair, then we held onto each other in our tears and anguish and the light began to enter.

In a sense, what I give to people is given back to me in different ways. Paul Tillich wrote, "Care is essentially mutual: the one who gives care also receives care."[2] Then it would not surprise you to learn that not long after this incident, I became a hospice chaplain and later an Anglican parish priest.

Gordon Hilsman was my CPE supervisor. He often shared stories of his time as a chaplain to reinforce our learning. One story stuck with me, long after the training was over. He was a chaplain resident in a small-town hospital in the upper Midwest. A young couple had twin boys, but one died shortly after birth.

How do parents meet that situation? What do they feel when the best time in their life is right next to the worst—the birth of one child and the death of the other?

Here is the story in his own words:

"I was called to that room almost immediately by a nurse. I entered the room unable to imagine what to say. I don't actually remember saying what I did, or the brief conversation after. But several months later, the husband—a slender, bearded, tough and intelligent looking man in his early thirties—appeared in the town grocery line immediately in front of me. He glanced back and I knew he recognized me as the chaplain on that day.

I said I remembered him from the day his infant son died.

He hesitated, and then said, "Yeah. You know, you said that day the only thing you could have said that I wouldn't have thrown you out of the room!"

"What did I say?" I asked.

His reply: "You just said, 'This makes no sense at all.'"

Somehow my words had hit the tragic wound in just about the right spot for the human connection to take place. The man's grief was not healed—it never will be, totally. But somebody had seen the hurt and dared to mention it, in the hospital room and in the grocery line. The worst pains are intimate. They require intimate words, and actions, which only rarely seem to come. As caregivers on the spot, we need to dare making them come more often."

What Gordon describes is confrontation as intimate words and actions in painful situations. Walking with empathy alongside someone in their suffering is the essence of spiritual care. If we are able to do so when they are traumatized by shock or violence, the benefit to them (and possibly bystanders) can be enormous—more than we can even know.

Chaplains are found in hospitals, hospices, the military, and other occupations, but I have also found that we can be standing in line at *Starbucks,* listening to the story of the person ahead of us, and they quickly come to trust you, because you are really listening. And their heart pours out, and you find yourself in spiritual care.

Why does that happen? Because what we have learned does not stop when we walk out of the hospital? No, it informs our very lives and spills out spontaneously, if we are willing.

Contact Info: The Rev Dr Joel C Graves, DMin, ACPE, retired hospice chaplain and Anglican pastor. Author of *Leadership Paradigms in Chaplaincy.* www.JoelGraves.com

[1] Henri J. M. Nouwen, *The Wounded Healer—Ministry in Contemporary Society* (New York: Image Books Doubleday, 1979)

[2] Antoinette Pinto-Sequiera, *Walking on Holy Ground: With Persons Suffering from the Alzheimer's Disease* (Glendale: Aion Multimedia, 2014), referencing Paul Tillich quote.

Chapter Eleven:

The Unsheltered Wanderer
by
Rod Seeger with Gordon J Hilsman

Jesus' words, "The poor you have always with you," easily ring in your ears as you walk such streets as the Haight Asbury section of San Francisco or downtown Los Angeles. They are everywhere, unsheltered wanderers who may proudly refer to themselves as the "last free people" left. From a caregiving point of view however, they are a conglomerative mixture of combat "wounded warriors," sadly addicted stumblers, romantically discouraged loners, tragically sad grievers, and some destitute, unsophisticated people who have never been habilitated into society. Their spiritual struggles that intertwine with their heroic mutual generosity and unconscionable cruelty to one another quietly fester, chronically inaccessible to anyone who attempts to lighten their burdens.

The Rev Rod Seeger has done his part to dip a cup of mercy into that sea of need. Seeing that milieu as a hotbed of potential learning for budding pastors and other spiritual care neophytes, he established a clinical pastoral education program there that has both cared for and learned from hundreds of unsheltered wanderers since 2014. He knows how the chaotic streets frequently require confrontation, in combination with patient listening, to plant seeds of care in situations of overwhelming personal and interpersonal need.

In 2014 I began developing a CPE (Clinical Pastoral Education) program at the San Francisco Night Ministry. That program has been providing spiritual care to people living and working on the streets since 1964. Typically, a night minister walks the streets of San Francisco from 10 pm to 4 am every night of the year. The night minister meets and greets people while walking in areas of San Francisco where people are living on or working on the streets. Since the program has been in place for over fifty years, the night minister is known to people living or working on the streets as a non-judgmental, accepting, caring person, who people can safely talk to. Several people serve as the night minister, so people are aware that it may be a different person who they meet at night. They also know the person will be non-judgmental, accepting, and caring. Setting up the CPE program was an experiment to see if the "CPE model" of teaching and learning would work effectively in this setting. After conducting just one twenty-week part-time program, it was clear that CPE would function effectively in the teaching and learning of providing spiritual care to people who were in need and in crisis. The outcomes of what are part of a CPE program were easily addressed in this first CPE program. Therefore, teaching and learning clarification, support and confrontation, was a regular part of the ongoing experience of those who participated in the CPE program. By 2017 the CPE program was fully accredited and providing extended and full-time CPE. The clinical hours were fulfilled walking the streets at night as a night minister, leading worship at

Open Cathedral twice each week, answering phones on the Care Line which was every night from 10 pm to 2 am, and participating in a support group/bible study group once each week. In all these settings, confrontation was an important skill to have and was used regularly in each of these settings.

Becoming Courageous, Comfortable and Skilled with Confronting

In providing spiritual care with people living on the streets, clarification, support, and confrontation are three skills that are essential for the caregivers to practice. For many people and neophyte caregivers, especially pastors without clinical education, confrontation is looked down upon, frowned upon, and avoided at all costs. But in street ministry confrontation is an important skill to have and to know when to use it. There are times when what we learned in our families is that confrontation is bad and wrong. Also, in our families we may have learned that the only way to confront another person is to get in their face and scream and holler at them. This style of confrontation was used only when all else fails. Part of learning how to confront another person in a healthy manner means needing to look at what we have learned about how to confront. We also need to discover whatever attitudes we have about using confrontation. We also need to discover the many ways to confront another.

What follows are examples of when confrontation is necessary in providing spiritual care and various ways to confront another person. I like to think of confrontation as thesis, antithesis, synthesis. We use actual situations as hypothetical to practice what it feels like to find words to meet new, unique, and challenging care situations.

Confronting a Person Whose Perception of a Situation has Dangerously Broken with Reality

Confrontation is important when the caregiver needs to challenge, correct, or intervene with a person, if their behavior is dangerous to themselves or to others. The caregiver needs to be able to assess the situation and discern if confrontation is needed.

I recall one night walking down Market Street in San Francisco with a CPE student. Someone yelled at us from across the street that there was a man with a gun, and we needed to duck for cover. Obviously, we heeded that advice. While seeking safety behind a large mailbox we peeked around the corner of the mailbox and saw no one with a gun. We saw the man who had yelled at us. He was also hiding behind a large container. We saw that he was afraid, and he continued to warn us. When we saw there was no one with a gun we made our way over to him. As we began talking with him, we saw he was in extreme distress. He told us of various things he saw that were dangerous around us. We did not see any. We decided that it would be best to call for assistance to help him get help for his delusions. We explained to him we did not see what he was seeing. No one was going to shoot him. We decided he needed some help from mental health professionals and not continue living on the streets. His fear was real. The man with a gun was not. This was causing him stress that needed to be taken care of.

We gently confronted his perception of what he thought was real. We used such phrases as, "Sir, we aren't seeing what you're seeing. You are clearly fearful right now. We want you to know that we can protect you for right now and that there is help for you to come. For now, it is important that you not act too quickly. You'll be safe with us right now." We assisted him in getting help.

Confronting a Person Who is a Danger to Self

Sometimes if a person is in danger to self and is putting self into harm's way, the caregiver needs to intercept the person by confronting their behavior. I encountered a woman whose baby had just died. She said she just wanted to kill herself. She was not married. She was not in a relationship with a man. She simply wanted a baby, so she got pregnant. The baby was born premature and was in an intensive care nursery for several weeks before the baby died. When I met her, she was waiting for the baby to be released to a mortuary for burial. She was waiting for that to happen before she would kill herself. We talked for a long time about the plans she had for her and her baby. She talked about wanting to see her baby one more time. She wanted to go to the mortuary and see her baby one last time. I asked if I could accompany her. She agreed.

At the mortuary we saw her little baby. She was sad and hurt. After a while we left the mortuary and walked to where she was staying. As we walked and talked, I asked her, "Are you still thinking of killing yourself?" She replied "Yes." I asked her about her plan to kill herself. She said it would not be right away because she needed to wrap up a number of loose strings, including plans she had already made for her baby. She had already enrolled her in daycare and pre-school and other activities. She needed to cancel all of these arrangements. We continued to talk. After a while we parted ways. Several months later I heard she had moved to Portland to live with her sister.

I knew I needed to confront her about her thoughts and plans to kill herself. I wanted to let her know I cared about her. I confronted her gently. I wanted her to talk about what was going on with her without any judgments so she would not feel all alone with the death of her daughter.

Confronting a Person Hurting Another

If a person is threatening another, it may be necessary to intervene by confronting the perpetrator. When one person is physically harming another, it often needs someone to confront the aggressor. This can be tricky.

As is demonstrated in the Karpman Triangle,[1] a rescuer who intervenes in a situation where the victim is being abused by a perpetrator, the dynamic can quickly shift, and the rescuer becomes the victim.

One night when two CPE students were walking in the Tenderloin District, they spotted a group of five or six men kicking a man who was on the sidewalk. When they spotted this, they knew they needed to confront the situation. They also knew these men could turn on them and they would become the victims. One CPE student noticed a police car parked on the opposite side of the intersection. She immediately ran to the police car and told them what was happening. She implored the police to intervene. The police car immediately sped over to where the men were. Within a minute or two, three other police cars arrived. Upon seeing the police, the men dispersed in every direction. The man who had been beaten slowly got up and began to walk away. The CPE students attempted to converse with him. He continued to walk away and did not respond to them. Discretion is the better part of valor, but can a caregiver really abandon a person actively being attacked?

Confronting a Person Making Disturbances and Being Distracting

In more mild exchanges, such as in outdoor worship time, it may be necessary to confront a person who is making disturbances and distracting people from worshipping. In conversations on the street when several people are together, confronting someone who is routinely interrupting an activity or conversation may be required. More often at first, an attempt is made to reason with a person. If that fails it may be necessary to confront them. Any of these confrontations could be simply talking directly with a person, suggesting an alternate behavior to what has been happening.

Confronting a Person Blatantly Manipulating in Ridicule of a Minor Authority

Len was a retired physician in his mid-sixties, volunteering as a CPE student in a food and shelter facility in Tacoma, Washington. On one of Len's first days volunteering, a raggedly dressed man who he's seen being boisterous that day, approached him and asked:

Man: "Hey buddy, can you get me a tarp? I got me some socks 'n stuff but it's rainin' and I ain't got no tarp. I'm gonna get soaked out there."

Chaplain Len: "No sir, I don't have tarps.

Man: "Heyyyyyy man, I could die out there."

C: "I'm really sorry, sir, but I don't give out tarps. I'm a chaplain."

Man: "A chap what? Ain't you staff?"

C: "I am. But I'm a chaplain. I listen to people and support them, sometimes pray with them, ask questions."

Man: Begins yelling, making a scene, cursing, berating. A small crowd gathers.

C: Remains calm, maintains the slightly vulnerable look that normally characterizes him, in silence. A few minutes later, after the small crowd has dispersed, the wanderer returns, slips up behind the chaplain, touches his arm and speaks quietly.

Man: "You done good pastor. You done real good. If you'd a got me anything, you'd be the 'tarp guy', the 'get stuff guy', the 'give stuff out guy' around here. But you ain't. You're lots better than that. I was testin' ya, like I do most all the new chaplains. You done good!"

Saying no is sometimes a quality confrontation that subtly teaches.

On the streets the night minister is largely perceived as someone to be respected which makes it important for the night minister to be able to confront people when needed.

Contact Info: Rod Seeger, MDiv, Street Chaplain Educator, ACPE Certified Educator, Retired RodSeeger@aol.com

[1] Stephen B. Karpman, *A Game Free Life: The definitive book on the Drama Triangle and Compassion Triangle* (San Francisco: Drama Triangle Publications: 2014).

Chapter Twelve:

The Bereft: Beckoning Forth the Grief
by
Fr John Bucchino

Since Kubler Ross's 1964 book On Death and Dying, the first widely read modern-era book on grieving, hundreds of books have instructed all of us about every major loss from a beloved infant to a breakup with a teenaged lover. Yet still we die, 60% in acute care hospitals, 20% in nursing homes, and only 20% where most of us say we want to end our lives—at home. Many of us still die alone, often with no concentrated interpersonal attention to the confusing and scary sensations and thoughts within us. We all experience several major losses during our lifetime and grieve most of them in isolation, even from those who love us deeply. Most counselors and psychotherapists advertise that they specialize in grief work among other issues. Yet hospitals are full of people who carry with them prior grief, the sad, warm, sentiments and even fears that accompany major loss.

What is the role of confrontation in teasing out worries and reminiscences, and sorting the values that ease the experience of major loss and dying? Fr. John Bucchino, a Catholic priest pastor, hospital chaplain, and clinical pastoral educator, illustrates here the deft listening, intuitive grasping, and sensitive responding that it takes to simply care for real people grieving real losses, past, anticipated, and immediate.

THE STORY OF MRS. KELLY: Intricate Confrontation in the Context of Grieving

I visited Mrs. Kelly as her chaplain during each of her four hospitalizations at the end of her life. She was an 80-year-old Irish-born woman, a staunch Roman Catholic and a devoted grandmother to her grandchildren with whom she lived. I noticed that in each of the four visits which were spaced out over six months, there was a deterioration in her physical health and in her emotional well-being. The physical side was less freedom in being able to move around and care for herself. The emotional sign was mentioning that she was feeling less needed by her family and more of a burden to them.

It was quite apparent that she was in a state of grieving the losses of these precious parts of her life; even anticipating death by some of the words she said, and the downward spiraling in her feelings of hope. I got to know her as a person of inner strength, who was always most comfortable caring for others rather than asking for care.

In trying to assist Mrs. Kelly's grieving process, I found her needing to stay in charge of her life while holding onto the role of matriarch so she could fulfill her felt duty to care for her grandchildren. I experienced her as wanting to stay in charge of the visit with me, not really letting me in easily to touch her emotional/spiritual pain. My approach was to listen to her fears and recognize her anger. I took on a supportive presence, respecting the grief she was experiencing.

Each time I visited her, it always felt like the very first visit. I experienced her formality towards me as both cultural and yet as a way to protect her anger from showing.

> Patient: "Oh it is good that a chaplain is coming to visit me; I can use confession!" (Said with a heaviness of spirit). After telling me a bit more about how she had been handling her physical decline and family relationships each time, I sensed that her presenting issue of wanting confession was really covering over something deeper. So I thought after my own self-re-introduction, this time I would "dive into" an exploration of her underlying emotional heaviness.

> Chaplain: "You seem burdened by something that is weighing on you, Mrs. Kelly." She took that statement from me as a way to talk about her perceived sins and shortcomings in life, directing our dialogue to her wrongdoings while expressing guilt.

> P: "I wasn't a good Catholic. I didn't always attend Mass. I didn't trust in God much. And I was unfaithful in my prayer life..." I did not assess that her guilt was the primary concern, even though she continued in that direction of presenting her specific wrongdoings. The heaviness of spirit did not leave her. Her manner of confessing in this way

felt like a shield protecting her from facing something more at the core of her troubled spirit. Was it really guilt or anger turned against herself? Going with the flow of listening to her list of perceived sins, I waited for the right moment to explore her grief at a deeper level:

C: "Mrs. Kelly, I see that you are in great distress over your wrongdoings; yet, you sound quite upset with yourself."

P: "Well, yes. Whenever someone is unfaithful in not doing their obligations, that offends God." The tone she expressed with the word "obligations" carried emotional weight.

C: "Wow, I can hear how being such a very devoted person to God you would naturally feel some disappointment with yourself."

P: "Yes, chaplain; it is the way I was brought up, and the way I have practiced my belief all my life!"

C: "There sounds like some anger at yourself for not living up to your belief. How do you feel about facing God one day having these feelings towards yourself?"

P: "Oh yes, God is certainly merciful; but I have done this over and over again and......I am not so sure God is happy with me!" She repeats some of her failings in life.

C: "Yes, I can hear your uncertainty and distress about facing God!"

P: Remains silent, then says, "Yes chaplain, you are right!"

C: "Yet some of the obligations that you told me that you failed in, were really not your fault!"

I repeated some of the experiences from her life that I remembered she had shared with me, starting with how she was abandoned by the men in her life: her father at her young age when he abandoned the family, and her husband when he died early on in their marriage, forcing her to take on the role of family matriarch, feeling overly responsible for the family. How then years later, then Grandma Kelly came to the U.S. as an immigrant with her family and continued in her role as matriarch. She made a promise to God that she would never abandon them as she had been abandoned. As the years passed, she became more frail and was unable to care for them as she had done previously.

This brought us then to the present, with her acknowledging how she is taking out her frustration on them. She did not want to face what she called her "failure" to fulfill her obligation. In the last visit we had, I challenged this self-judgment about not being able to fulfill her role. How could she fulfill such a monumental responsibility with so few resources in her life? I focused with her on her belief in the "God of Obligations" rather than in the "God of

Mercy," using some quotes from St. Paul's contrast between law-based faith versus love-based faith that Jesus called her to. Yet I felt that her sense of "obligation" was deeply engrained in her and well-defended.

She was admitted to the hospital and I had a final visit with her. Early in the conversation, I said:

>C: "Mrs. K., I was wondering if you ever considered that due to your illness, your role in life might have changed?"
>
>P: Looking puzzled. "What do you mean? Aren't I still responsible for my grandchildren and great-grandchildren?"
>
>C: "Well, yes you are. And I believe you can still fulfill it in an even more effective way—and even while you are ill." My theory told me to join her resistance rather than fight it.
>
>P: "What do you mean?"
>
>C: "Have you considered that now you may have a new obligation to fulfill for your family?"
>
>P: Very attentive. "And what is that?
>
>C: "That you, as a faith-filled matriarch, might want your children and grand-children to experience what a good dying might look like!"

P: With curiosity. "Tell me more about that!"

C: "Well, I believe that your faith is so important to you and to your family as well. By you showing them with much confidence and trust how you believe that God would be welcoming you home, you can let go of your obligations with relief. And that you would show to your grandchildren that you not only trust God, but also trust them to continue your role as a caring grandmother."

P: Pondering. "I've never thought of a good dying."

C: Wondering if what I offered helped her. "How are you feeling about what I'm offering to you, Mrs. K.?"

P: She seemed lighter in spirit. "You've given me a lot to think about, chaplain. Thank you."

We said our good-byes, and I told her I would pray for her and visit her again. But I did not see her again before she was discharged from the hospital the next day. Two weeks later one, of her granddaughters called me at my office to tell me that her grandmother died and thanked me for helping her to die in a very peaceful emotional state.

Contact Info: Fr. John Bucchino, MDiv, Parish Pastor and ACPE Certified Educator, Manchester NH jocchi2@aol.com

Chapter Thirteen:

The Dying: Confronting as a Tool in End-of-Life Spiritual Care
by
The Rev Timothy Shipe, MDiv, BCC

There are fewer more frightening and impactful confrontations in life than being told your life is ending. One topic of discussion many people avoid is death and dying. Hospice workers often have the familiar experience of sharing about where they work, and hear some form of: "Oh, I could never do that!" Similarly, one topic of discussion most Clinical Pastoral Education (CPE) students prefer to sidestep is the notion of confronting others. Even among more seasoned spiritual care providers such as pastors and chaplains, when it comes to confronting others, the response is often familiar: "Oh, I could never do that!" If done skillfully, however, confrontation can be a useful tool within spiritual care in a variety of settings. This chapter presents the prescriptive use of confrontation as a valuable tool in end-of-life spiritual care with hospice patients and their family/friends, but could pertain to the chaplain's relationship with interdisciplinary care team colleagues as well.

A primary goal of spiritual care in healthcare chaplaincy is relationships, whether it be facilitating, initiating, enhancing, restoring, transforming and/or, especially in the case of end-of-life spiritual care, successfully concluding them well. Given that spirituality is about connection and that there is much that isolates care-recipients within a healthcare setting, another important goal of spiritual care is assisting care-receivers in strengthening trust: trust of self and others, which includes the divine/transcendent.

Attachment theory has long asserted the notion that human beings are social creatures and therefore hardwired for relationship.[1] In the absence of relationships, human development, growth and healing are stymied. In addition, research highlights the importance of quality relationships.[2] It has been documented that patients who have greater trust in their healers tend to have better health outcomes.[3] For this reason, when entering the patient's room, the chaplain should note areas of both connection and disconnection within the experience of the care-receiver(s) and between the care-receiver and their care-givers.

In his book, *Spiritual Care In Common Terms: How Chaplains Can Effectively Describe the Spiritual Needs of Patients in Medical Records*, Gordon Hilsman writes:

> "The inherently uncontrollable nature of hospitalization outcomes causes virtually anybody immersed in healthcare culture to experience in some measure an underlying impression of heightened human

vulnerability. For patients it begins at admission or a bit before, when a sense of alarm affects the soul enough to motivate the drive to a facility or the phone call for help." [4]

In addition to acute vulnerability, there are a variety of experiences and feelings that can potentially hinder a patient's relationships with others, such as deep mistrust of self and/or others, shame, doubt, guilt, feeling inferior, loss of identity and familiar role, experiencing isolation, feeling stuck-ness/disempowerment and despair.[5] When the chaplain's spiritual assessment detects that one of these experiences and/or feelings is isolating a dying patient, a prescriptive use of confrontation may be necessary in order to facilitate more effective connection between a dying patient and their caregivers. The following story provides an example.

Confronting Patients

Lester (not his real name) arrived to the twenty-bed hospice with his guitar and a large three-ring notebook filled with songs he had written. He was more interactive than many patients who came to the in-patient unit. Visitors and staff alike were often treated to an impromptu concert, as he perched on the edge of his bed strumming his guitar. In his first days on the unit, Lester sang songs that were hopeful, positive and described his vision of God as forgiving and just. From his presentation and music, the chaplain observed that he was a person of deep Christian faith and was very trusting of his Creator.

In an initial meeting, the chaplain became curious as to why a person who appeared very positive and upbeat, without a care in the world, was attached to three pain pumps. Experience in hospice teaches that when a patient has that much pain medication going into their body, the interdisciplinary care team is chasing more than just physical pain. Utilizing a spiritual assessment framework, the chaplain initially assessed that the patient was experiencing formidable relatedness pain between himself and his care team.[6] The incongruence of the patient telling others that he was "fine" and the amount of pain medication he was being given to help bring some relief, led the chaplain to wonder about how much Lester trusted the care of others and how much of his body, mind and spirit he felt like he could open to the dynamic care of his hospice team.

Initial conversation with Lester remained surface-level as he shared well-rehearsed religious platitudes (i.e. "God is good!" and "I am blessed!"). He proved adept at removing focus from himself by asking the chaplain questions about himself and about the work of a hospice chaplain.

During the third visit, sensing that the care team was not able to address or care for any of the patient's non-physical pain due to his hesitancy to risk and trust, the chaplain decided to confront Lester. The following is a paraphrase of the interaction:

> Chaplain: "Lester, I have appreciated your willingness to share about your faith and trust in God, but I wonder if there isn't more to the story?"

Patient: "What do you mean?"

C: "In hospice, we care for the whole person:- mind, body and spirit. Most people who come here struggle with more than just physical pain. Many also struggle with emotional and spiritual pain."

P: Nervously. "Yea?"

C: "I couldn't help but notice that you have three pain pumps connected to you. In my experience, that much medication means there is more than just physical pain stirring within. I don't think it is just your body that is hurting."

P: Silence. Tears well up. "I have been hurting for a long time…"

Lester went on to share deep, raw residual grief from having been molested as a child and losing his only brother, who was also molested, to death by suicide. As if that were not enough tragedy, Lester eventually became a parent and molested his daughter. What lay just under the surface of his outward positivity was formidable guilt, shame and terror as Lester went on to confide that he was ultimately fearful that his "heavenly Father" would do to him what his earthly father had done.

As the chaplain listened to his painful life story, he began to see that Lester was too afraid and filled with shame to be authentic. What the chaplain initially assessed as relatedness pain between himself and others expanded to include deep and raw relatedness pain between the patient and his father, between the patient and his deceased brother, between the patient and his daughter, and between the patient and the divine.

Lester was also carrying palpable meaning pain (i.e. "What have I done with my life?", "What kind of father have I been?"), forgiveness pain (i.e. "How could I hope to even look at my daughter again and be forgiven?", "If you think what my earthly father did was bad, wait until I am before my heavenly Father!") and hopelessness pain (i.e. "I am destined for Hell!").[7] He hid behind positivity and optimism, because he feared the judgement of others and, therefore, suffered deeply and alone.

The chaplain's confrontation with Lester in his words, "I couldn't help but notice...I don't think it is just your body that is hurting," opened the door for Lester to speak the unspeakable and to participate more fully in relationship, with me, with others and with the transcendent/divine. By the time Lester died several days later, he authentically and courageously opened more of himself to care, reducing the three pain pumps down to one.

Another occasion to use confrontation as a tool in spiritual care at the end of life arises when confronting a patient's sense of wretchedness, being worthless and/or unforgiveable. In his book, *The Theory and Practice of Group Psychotherapy*, Irvin Yalom comments that many individuals in need of healing and a therapeutic process suffer from the *"disquieting thought that they are unique in their wretchedness, that they alone have certain frightening or unacceptable problems, thoughts, impulses, and fantasies."*[8] Learning that others have similar thoughts, inclinations and experiences can diminish a feeling of isolation. By normalizing some stories and experiences, the chaplain aims to foster a deep and profound sense of inclusion. There are times when the chaplain will choose to confront the assumptions made by patients about how spiritual care functions within the institution that the chaplain serves, as well as assumptions about the chaplain themselves. It is not uncommon for a patient to decline the chaplain's offer of a visit by saying, "I am not religious." Although it is true that not everyone has a religion, effective spiritual care in the context of healthcare chaplaincy presumes that everyone has a human spirit and that spirit is impacted by disease and diagnosis, especially when the diagnosis is terminal.

Confronting Families

A familiar experience for many healthcare chaplains is being contacted by a patient's family member and being asked to "save" the patient before they die, referring to a widely used concept within the Judeo-Christian faith tradition. However, the healthcare chaplain has a different care contract and care relationship with patients than a pastor, Rabbi or Imam have with members of their own spiritual community.

Confronting assumptions about what the chaplain does provides an opportunity to gently yet firmly educate about what spiritual care can be. The chaplain's spiritual care of patients and/or families might involve reading and suggesting various sacred writings, prayer and other rituals. But it may also include shared reminiscing people and experiences of the past, imagining or reimagining the future, reflective meaning-making regarding the diagnosis or prognosis, or may even be casual banter on the restoration of cars or performance of the local sports teams.

The chaplain might also confront what may be referred to as the presumed location of greatest spiritual need, by redirecting where or to whom their spiritual care is offered. The following vignette illustrates an example:

> Family Member: "Chaplain, would you please stop by and speak with my mom? The doctor said that she is 'close.'"
>
> Chaplain: "I would be happy to check in on your mom. It sounds like what the doctor said really impacted you."
>
> FM: "Yes. I don't want my mom to die before she gets right with Jesus. She was never baptized. I tried to speak with her about it for years. She just never followed through."
>
> C: "It sounds like this has caused you a lot of grief and sadness over the years. And now you have been told that your mom will likely die soon…more sadness and grief. Am I right in detecting some fear?"
>
> FM: "Well yes! I want her to go to heaven. If she does not confess Jesus as Lord, she will not be allowed by God into heaven. That is what my tradition says. She will listen to you."

C: "It sounds like you are afraid to lose her twice…once soon to death and then potentially for all eternity."

FM: "Exactly. That's my mom."

C: "I hear your sadness and your fear of losing her. Thank you for sharing that. Part of my role here is to meet people where they are at [sic], often in deep sadness and fear. As a Chaplain I have a different kind of care relationship than a priest or pastor has with parishioners."

FM: "Oh."

C: "When someone is in the hospital, it is usually more than just the body that hurts. When you were sharing, there seemed to be some hurt. If you have time, I would like to hear more about that."

At that point, the family member has options that include dismissing the chaplain or accepting the invitation to share more about their own hurt. If the family member accepts the invitation, the chaplain can then offer options for working with the family member that include: acknowledging and processing grief, imagining what comes next after the death of the family member's loved one, acknowledging and processing the relatedness pain between family member and patient, as well as any potential meaning and hopelessness pain stirring within the family member. They may also offer prayer/ritual with the family member and may further educate about the role of the chaplain and provide potential referrals for the family member. The gentle yet firm confrontation by the chaplain can honor the patient and family member by suggesting that they each may have differing spiritual needs and resources.

Other instances of utilizing confrontation as a tool in end-of-life spiritual care include efforts by the Chaplain to diminish emotional and/or spiritual distance between the patient and their loved ones. This might involve confronting family members whose "hovering" may be overwhelming a weakened patient with their anxiety and frenetic energy.

It may also involve confronting family members who want to avoid talking about death, intending to protect the patient and not cause additional emotional harm when the patient clearly expresses a desire to talk more openly and courageously about how to bring closure to their life.

There might also be situations when it is appropriate to confront family members who wish to debate advanced directives and wills at bedside in the final hours of a patient's life. Such conversations (or lack of conversation regarding death) at unhelpful times, can lead to a sense of further emotional hurt and disconnection between patients and their loved ones.

Confronting Interdisciplinary Care Team Colleagues

Just as it is necessary to confront inaccurate assumptions by patients and loved ones about what spiritual care is and how it functions within a healthcare context, it can be necessary to occasionally confront fellow interdisciplinary care colleagues about their attitudes and assumptions regarding spiritual care and the role of the chaplain. The chaplain frequently hears from another member of the care team, "They don't need a chaplain. They are not religious." Such moments are opportunities to not only educate care colleagues about the benefits of spiritual care, but are also opportunities for the chaplain to lift up and highlight the patient's humanity in the midst of very technical and medically-laden jargon that often dominates descriptions of patients in medical facilities. Such an intervention by the chaplain can facilitate a new or renewed connection between the patient and members of their care team.

Another example of confronting interdisciplinary care colleagues is when the chaplain hears a member of the patient's care team say, "There is nothing else we can do." Such a sentiment can further isolate patients from their care team, because patients and/or their loved ones often feel like the care team is giving up on them. Such a sentiment can potentially cause discord between interdisciplinary team members themselves by insinuating that hospice and/or palliative care is an inferior service area. The interdisciplinary care team can always pursue and provide the best care possible, given the circumstances, while striving to keep the patient as comfortable and connected as possible.

Another familiar phrase the chaplain can confront is when care team colleagues talk about "withdrawing life support." The chaplain can provide thoughtful education about communicating a kinder and more empowering phrase such as "allow natural death." The notion of withholding something from a patient is not only distressing to medical professionals, but the idea of withholding or taking away something from a loved one can cause deep sadness, grief, regret and palpable guilt within surviving family members, even years later. Reflecting back on the event, surviving family will likely feel more positive about their efforts to care and advocate for their loved one when able to recall what they "allowed" rather than what was "withheld."

Contact Info: The Rev. Timothy Shipe, MDiv, BCCi, ACPE Certified Educator, Harborview Medical Center, Seattle WATShipe@uw.edu

[1] Bowlby, John. "Maternal care and mental health," *Bulletin of the World Health Organization*, 3, 3, 355-533, (1968).
 I highly recommend Bowlby's *Attachment and Loss: 3 Volumes,* available from Basic Books.

[2] Umberson D, Montez JK. (2010). "Social relationships and health: a flashpoint for health policy." *Journal of Health and Social Behavior,* 51 Suppl, (2010), S54-S66. doi:10.1177/002 2146510383501

[3] Birkhäuer J, et al. (2017). "Trust in the health care professional and health outcome: a meta-analysis." *PLOS One,* 12, 2, e0170988, (February 7, 2017). doi:10.1371/journal.pone.0170988

[4] Gordon J. Hilsman, *Spiritual Care in Common Terms: How Chaplains Can Effectively Describe the Spiritual Needs of*

Patients in Medical Records (Philadelphia: Jessica Kingsley Publisher, 2017), 29

[5] My spiritual assessment framework has been enhanced and informed by insights from Erikson's human development theory. I especially recommend, Erik Erikson, *Identity and the Life Cycle* (New York: W.W. Norton & Co, 1994) revised edition.

[6] Richard Groves and Henriette Anne Klauser, *The American Book of Living and Dying: Lessons in Healing Spiritual Pain* (Berkley: Celestial Arts, 2009). Part of my spiritual assessment framework includes the four areas of spiritual pain (relatedness pain, forgiveness pain, meaning pain and hopelessness pain).

[7] Groves, ibid.

[8] Irvin D. Yalom, *The Theory and Practice of Group Psychotherapy* (New York: Perseus Books Group, 2005), 6

PART THREE:

Confronting in Professional Practice

Chapter Fourteen:

How to Confront Your Organizational Superior
by
Jill Rasmussen-Baker

Some needed confrontations involve factors that add even more peril for chaplains than others. They involve potential loss of their job, their livelihood, even their career. Few administrators at any level comprehend the value and complexity of clinical pastoral education. They have no way of estimating this value except their experience and your reputation. Yet their material support is essential for you to carry out your role as a spiritual clinician or clinical educator.

As director of spiritual care at Harborview Medical Center in Seattle, associated with the University of Washington, Jill Rasmussen has learned how to stand face-to-face with her administrator, to whom she reports, and even the CEO, to whom her administrator reports. Drawing examples from her service there and at previous hospitals, she describes her methods clearly here. (The term "superior" means the person to whom she immediately reports in the organization, varying with her changes in employment at various facilities over the years).

As the youngest of six siblings, I have historically been more compliant and submissive with my organizational superiors, as I was with my parents. My next older sibling and I were told by our older siblings that we "weren't planned." Early in life I "knew" that my parents' hands were already more than full, and they were already challenged emotionally, financially, and physically with hardships beyond my comprehension before I came into being. In the midst of these messages, many unspoken, I did my best to get my needs met by asking as little as possible of my parents, now deceased, with whom I always had strong relationships. I have done personal work in my own Clinical Pastoral Education, in therapy, and in other growth-filled education and experiences to develop assertiveness, including speaking up for my own and others' needs. While I grew in assertiveness, I see that my upbringing prepared me quite well in simultaneously maintaining important relationships, including with my superiors. I'm grateful for admirable leaders, mentors, and educators at Harborview and elsewhere, several included in my sharing here, about whose positive impact on my professional and personal learning and growth, I could write an entire book.

Foundations: Building Trust and Rapport

As with my other relationships, I have found that confronting my organizational superior has been best received when I have earned their trust and developed positive rapport with them. I have developed particular practices in building rapport: discovering, and reporting on, what's important; minimizing surprises; providing reliable information on issues; and seeking consultation from my superior when it's appropriate.

First, I find it helpful here to pay attention to, and to find out, what's important to my superior and to the organization. If there are key values or concepts important to this person/organization, I often present regular, e.g. weekly or monthly, updates using these values/concepts as my outline, reporting each update detail under one of these categories. For example, in an organization where service to the patient was a key value, when I worked with Volunteer Services and Interpreter Services to add a Muslim volunteer as a community spiritual care practitioner to serve our patients, I reported this update under "Serving the Patient" in my monthly one-to-one meeting, for which I provide a written agenda.

Second, minimizing surprises comes from my own not liking unwelcome surprises. I seek to anticipate what I would want to be kept informed of, if I were in my superior's role, and I seek to be the first to share with that superior, news that I expect they will hear elsewhere. For example, when an issue gets reported in our safety reporting system that needs to be investigated and/or addressed by our department, I am proactive in telling my superior about the issue.

Third, I not only tell my superior about such issues, I provide pertinent information, often in successive reports as new information becomes available, such as what I'm doing to investigate, what is causing the issue, and what others and/or I are/am doing to resolve the issue. For example, when my department was over budget at the beginning of the year due to predictable expenses early in the year that would not be experienced later in the year, I calculated when we would be back on budget, and I reported this to my boss. In a fiscal year starting in July, I communicated to my superior, "Due to our having an overlap of students on stipends for two weeks in August during orientation of incoming students, we are, as expected, over budget." I then shared how expenses would be lower in coming months due to a couple of factors, and I asserted, "We will be back on budget by January." We were, and my superior expressed trust in my fiscal reporting and planning.

Fourth, I build rapport by seeking consultation from my superior when it makes sense. For example, when I was concerned that a disappointing interpersonal interaction I reported to a colleague about this colleague's staff member wasn't being taken as seriously as I thought was optimal, I sought my superior's consultation on further actions, if any, that my superior recommend I take, such as reporting the issue to Human Resources (HR). "If this staff member, who routinely interacts with patients as part of their job treats me, a leader, this disappointingly," I noted, "I'm concerned that this person may treat patients similarly." When my superior, who hired this staff member years ago, said that reporting to HR was unnecessary after I shared my concern with the staff member's superior, I concluded that I'm not responsible for this staff member's actions or any risk they may pose; in doing this I was drawing on Bowen Family Systems Theory, also known as "Bowen Theory," in refraining from taking responsibility for something that is not my responsibility; in Bowen terms, I was refraining from over-functioning. While I was assertive with this staff member's superior about my concerns, I did not report this to HR. I was later affirmed by my superior for my handling of this issue that included my combination of assertiveness and restraint, and I believe that my consulting my superior strengthened our rapport.

Confrontation About Staffing: My Three-Part Approach

At a time when I was interim director of the Spiritual Care (SC) department of my institution, my Administrator shared that she and our Chief Executive Officer (CEO) were questioning the need and fiscal responsibility for our Clinical Pastoral Education (CPE) program and for having a director of the SC department. She asked me to use an SBAR (Situation-Background-Assessment-Recommendation) document to recommend and justify a department structure. After I vented my initial anger to trusted persons about the need to justify our department's resources (how can they not see our value?), I channeled my energy into creating a proposal that confronted this, and even my own, doubt of the need for our CPE program and for a department director.

First, as scary and vulnerable as it was to set aside my bias of valuing with passion both CPE and my role as a Certified Educator—certified in teaching CPE, setting aside my bias was an important step to prepare for exploring possible department structures. As my work progressed, I found the need for a three-part approach: the SBAR, testimony on patient and staff needs, and comparison with other medical centers.

In part one, the SBAR—after describing the Situation of this being an appropriate interim time to reflect on and explore this department's structure, I provided relevant historical and environmental Background, including financial pressures on the institution and replacement being scrutinized in every case of attrition. I also noted that we receive an average of 4.5 requests per night for spiritual care. I then provided assessment of four department structures that I imagined as most likely to work well given important factors, including number of patients, referrals, and current budget. Three of these included some form of a CPE program and one did not. The department in each imagined structure composed of at least twenty paid staff, including our seventeen part-time/occasional staff vital to our 24/7 coverage, and our more than fifty generous, valued volunteers. All of these imagined structures included a department director. For each of these four structures, I reflected on and listed pros and cons/risks, including implications to patients, to staff who receive spiritual care, to 24/7 on-site spiritual care, to SC department staff, and to budget. After careful consideration of these assessments and their risks and benefits, I concluded that the educational program was fiscally responsible and that having two certified educators was optimal for the vital service of our department's mission.

For part two—with patients at the heart of not only our organization's values but our department's service, I reached out to a number of leaders, including nurse managers and social workers, requesting statements about their perception of the value of spiritual care. Eleven lovely notes/letters/cards, including heart-wrenching stories, emotionally and anecdotally testified to our patients' need for 24/7 spiritual care as well as the importance to staff of our spiritual care *for them*. These stories and notes brought life to the average 4.5 requests for spiritual care per night and highlighted, as indisputable, the need for 24/7 on-site coverage.

In addition to the SBAR (part one) and the notes/cards/letters (part two), I added part three, a comparison that came from my own wondering about staffing levels of similar medical centers. I reached out to leaders of six medical centers nationwide that shared similarities, including in medical specialties with our medical center. I gathered such information as their staffing levels; their number of CPE residents and interns at various times of year, if any; and their number of patients. After estimating a Full-Time Equivalent (FTE) in staff/students for each institution, I used an Excel spreadsheet to help calculate the ratio of Spiritual Care Providers (SCP's) to patients for each institution and for each proposed department structure in my SBAR. I knew my organization wanted to be near average when compared with similar institutions. With all four department structures I proposed, an estimated ratio of SCP's to patient would be at or just below average when compared with these six similar institutions. I concluded that, of the four structures I proposed, the one with the most generous staffing, which was roughly at the average ratio and which had two Certified Educators, was fiscally responsible.

This spreadsheet (part three) confirmed that the two Certified Educators of most recent staffing levels empowered us to have SCP-to-patient ratios at or below the average when compared with these similar medical centers. Also, all but one of these other medical centers had 24/7 in-house SC coverage. Regarding the outlier, with the rest of us having ratings around three stars, as I noted in the SBAR, "I urge us NOT to follow their example, as (their) Medicare

Overall rating is one out of five stars, and their Medicare Patient Survey rating is two out of five stars."

After reading and reflecting on this three-part proposal (SBAR, notes/stories, and spreadsheet), my administrator, relaying feedback from her and our CEO, said, "This is impressive. We support the educational program and having a department director."

This proposal is another example of how I draw on Bowen Theory, in which the norm is to make decisions based on principles rather than reactions to feelings, such as in "fight or flight" situations. In this case, the proposal put forth principles of service for patients and fiscal responsibility. While I had feared losing the educational program and other resources and these feelings fueled my passion for creating a solid proposal, I don't think expressing these feelings to my administrator aloud or in the proposal would have been helpful. The cards and letters from hospital leaders and staff appealed to feelings, and included a disheartening patient story of when there wasn't an on-site SC Provider. I also included a story of heartfelt gratitude when medical staff were empowered to focus on their critical work with a patient in a code blue situation because an on-site SCP compassionately supported the needs of the understandably concerned family.

Confrontation When Data is not Available for Spiritual Care

Paying attention to the information sought in institutional decision-making is very important in confronting such arguments as justifying staffing levels. At one point, the medical center I was serving began working with a consulting organization that had benchmarks for a number of services provided by other healthcare organizations, including an average cost and range for particular services. I learned that my organization had a particular "target" such that we expected our costs to be a specific percentage of the average cost.

Aware that this consulting organization did not have benchmarks for spiritual care services, I came up with my own benchmark data using the Excel spreadsheet mentioned above. I brought this updated spreadsheet to my meeting with the budget administrator to whom my superior had delegated budget conversations in this particular meeting. In this meeting, the budget administrator said, "You know this is a very tight budget year. We're asking you and every leader to reduce expenses as much as possible, including labor expenses."

I handed this person my updated spreadsheet with benchmark data and responded, "Our Spiritual Care department is already meeting and even exceeding the (target) level when compared to Spiritual Care departments of similar medical centers, as you can see from the spreadsheet. To provide solid levels of patient care while being fiscally responsible, I see it appropriate for us to maintain our current level of staffing. If we reduce our staffing, we would go even further below the target level, putting our patient care at risk." "So you have assembled this data?" this administrator asked. "Yes," I said, "because (the consulting organization) does not have benchmarks for Spiritual Care, I have gathered this data from medical centers similar to ours to discern where we stand with Spiritual Care Provider-to-patient ratios, and I'm assessing that we already meet and even exceed the desired (target) level."

After further examination of the spreadsheet, this administrator said, "I see that you are already meeting the desired (target) level." I saw other non-revenue-generating departments lose staff that year and subsequent years. I think my creatively presenting the kind of data used by our institution to justify staffing, gave administrators what they needed to see that our Spiritual Care department continued to meet and even exceed the "target" level, and we did not lose staff.

Confrontation About Equity

"Don't waste an opportunity," is a phrase you may have heard. When the concept of equity was understandably used to decline a request I made, I used the concept of equity to bring more currency to a request that was on a back burner. Specifically, I had used information I'd gathered from other local medical centers to conclude that our pay for occasional Spiritual Care Providers (SCP's) was below the market level. My superior, agreeing that these rates should be increased, planned to request approval from the person to whom my superior reported. However, before this happened, there was a significant financial downturn, and I supported my superior's waiting for a more opportune time to request approval.

A few months later, I requested funding for flowers for a couple of staff members who, sadly, had each experienced the death of a close family member. In response, my superior wrote, "Let's talk about this. I have recently been concerned about the freer spending (of our department) compared to others. I think a well-worded card that you are so good at writing is generally what is expected. It is really an issue of equity as opposed to expense. Be interested in your thoughts."

After thoughtful reflection, I responded, drawing on the concept of equity, "I appreciate your thoughtful response. I am a fan of equity, and I don't want to propagate inequity across departments. I'm OK with not sending a gift beyond a card. I greatly appreciate your approval for us to put in the (current) budget, funding to make the pay rate for our (occasional SCP's) more equivalent to other medical centers in the area. I trust your judgment about when you think it's an appropriate time to request equity for our (occasional SCP's), who are making ($N/hour for day shifts), while (similar medical center SCP's) are making ($1.5 x N/hour for day shifts). I would appreciate our staying in touch about when it makes sense to bring these items forward to be addressed; I would like to see this at a time when you sense there's a high likelihood of approval/success. Thank you for all of your valued support of our department." I kept this initiative of equity in pay on my monthly meeting agenda with my superior, noting that I wanted this increase as soon as the financial climate was supportive. Within four months of the above email exchange regarding equity, I am grateful that my superior took this initiative to the person to whom my superior reported, and it was approved by all necessary levels.

Other Helpful Ideas, Including Lessons Learned

I have learned that it may be unhelpful to make an appeal based on feelings alone and that it can be helpful to be patient for results, to be patient in the timing of my giving confrontation, and to offer creative, alternate solutions.

While I highly value awareness of feelings and use of empathy in building rapport and other aspects of spiritual care, I learned through experience that making an appeal based on my feelings alone, especially on fear, did not get me the support I wanted. When space-planning leaders were sharing that organizations, including us in Spiritual Care would likely be moved to another area, I made a plea to my superior, stating, "I'm afraid that (particular service area impacted) and I will not receive the respect deserved, if the space allocated isn't as large as it is now." I was disappointed when later the draft grid of space allocation showed a decrease in space allocation for this (particular service area) and me. I had the impression that my superior had input into how space was allocated in this draft and that this superior had not valued my request.

After seeking consultation from an experienced colleague, a practice I often find helpful, I reached out directly to the space-planning leaders, cc'ing my superior, "I am writing to state the needs of (particular service area) and me in the space planning for the potential move to the (new location)." I then stated needs in terms of the number of persons to accommodate and the required furniture. After making this request based on work-related needs rather than my fears, I received an email from my superior, "This is well worded. Thank you." While this move did not happen in my time with that organization, I received a more supportive response from my superior when I focused, not on feelings, but on work-related needs.

I have found that the result of confrontation can take time and that it's helpful to be patient for results. On one occasion, I had been told in an initial conversation by someone working for the hiring organization, that an open position was of a particular level. It was after I had been hired and had taken the position, that I learned that the position was not of the stated level. After my first verbal plea to my superior, my superior said, "There was a miscommunication. At one time we had hoped that this position would be at (particular level), but that did not happen." I had a follow-up conversation with the initial person, who verified their understanding of the "particular level" communicated to me, and I provided a written statement to my superior, noting, "I see myself holding up my end in delivering everything I was expected to provide, and I'm asking that you hold up your end in delivering the (level) and corresponding benefits that were communicated to me before I was hired." In that written statement, I said, "I have spoken with (Name), who had understood and communicated that the position was at (particular level). While I am still unhappy with the response and I am considering gathering information from colleagues in similar roles, at this time I will continue to do the work I was hired to do, including (tasks with deadlines)." I acted with integrity in doing the work I was hired to do. A month or more later, I was called into a meeting with my superior and my superior's superior, who said, "I have fought for this and I was successful. We are giving you (particular level), and we are making it retroactive to your hire date." In this case, I think my patience was beneficial to my relationships with my superiors and to me.

Another time I found it helpful to be patient in the timing of my confrontation after my superior reprimanded me by email for not coming in during a weather emergency. My superior emailed, "Let's talk about it at our next meeting. All staff are essential personnel and expected to come in, albeit they might be late. It is especially important for leadership to set the bar. Finally, though spiritual care may be covered by other chaplains, you might be deployed elsewhere passing trays, sitting with a psych patient, etc. Thanks." Having not had a conversation earlier about these expectations, I was willing to plan more proactively to be on-site during weather emergencies going forward. However, I was disappointed and frustrated not to be asked what happened or to hear concern for my safety and well-being in my superior's communication. I waited patiently until our next scheduled meeting, when I brought a copy of this email, expressed my intention to plan more proactively going forward, and said, "I would have appreciated your asking what was happening for me or your showing concern for my safety in your communication." My superior acknowledged having room for improvement here and said that others had communicated similarly. I think my delaying to share this when I was beyond the peak of my frustration contributed to my superior's openly receiving my critique.

At times, when I'm saying, "No" to a request from my superior, I confront the request with a creative alternate solution. For example, one time a superior said, "I've talked with (Name). (Name) wants and needs CPE. It's important that we support (Name's) learning." In the screening process, including an interview, I assessed that this applicant wasn't ready for CPE, including giving and receiving the kind of constructive criticism that is helpful for

CPE learning. I assessed that I had time in my schedule to provide individual support to this applicant for their learning. Rather than saying a hard-stop "No" to my superior's request that I accept this student into CPE, I told my superior, "I think that it may be frustrating for both (Name) and for others in a CPE group with (Name) that (Name) isn't quite ready for giving and receiving critique and for other assignments and responsibilities that make for good learning. In order to provide (Name) a positive learning experience, I am willing to spend two hours individually with (Name) every other week having (Name) share about patient care, even in verbatims, so that I can support (Name's) learning and growth in an environment that is much lower stress than a CPE group." After reflection my superior said, "I like this idea. Let's talk to (Name)." Name agreed to this, a solution I believe was much better for all involved than my superior's original request.

Conclusion

In reflecting on helpful practices for confronting my superior, I have found it helpful to first develop foundational trust and rapport through such means as discovering and reporting on what's important, including to the organization; minimizing surprises; providing reliable information on issues, and seeking consultation from my immediate superior at appropriate times. When I was asked to recommend a department structure using an SBAR justification, I supplemented this with emotional and other appeals from staff for meeting patient and staff needs and with data comparing our staffing with similar medical centers. In other work in justifying staffing, I found it helpful to pay attention to benchmarking that was providing criteria for other departments, and I provided data that demonstrated similar benchmarking in analyzing and supporting our staffing levels.

When requested rate increases for particular Spiritual Care staff to achieve equity with the pay of similar local staff was, understandably delayed, I took advantage of my superior's raising the importance of equity in another area to bring attention to this inequity that was waiting for resolution.

I have learned that it's helpful not to confront based on feelings alone. I've also learned the value of being patient in waiting for desired results and in finding an appropriate time to confront, as well as the value of being creative in proposing alternate solutions.

In spiritual care, so much of our service is relational and is most effective when we have a strong alliance with the person with whom we are interacting. Experiencing interactions with my superior to be no exception, I have found that a positive relationship with my superior provides a helpful foundation for supportive and productive reception of my confrontation.

Contact Info: Jill Rasmussen-Baker, MDiv, Director of Pastoral Care, ACPE Certified Educator, Harborview UW Medical Center, Seattle WA calledtoserve@gmail.com

Chapter Fifteen:

Prophetic Pastoral Care of Confronting the Truth in Local Churches
by
Wayne Menking

Jesus was assumed to mostly be nice. But not always. And Paul of Tarsus was downright solidly critical with early Christian communities about their "factions", even in those earliest days of the Christian movement. Clinical Educator, Wayne Menking, has carried on that tradition actively for many years as a consultant to local churches in conflict. He describes here some of his interactions with people in engaging their church conflict for the hoped-for betterment of the congregations' future, not always neatly, but always at least partially successfully.

The prophetic and priestly care work of confrontation in a local congregation takes many forms. It can be the work of confronting a congregant with a behavior that is destructive to his family, to his employment, to his life, and perhaps even to the congregation. It can be the work of confronting a congregation with a condition or reality of its communal life and behavior that is adversely affecting its ability to live out its vocational mission to its community and the world. It can be the work of confronting powers within the congregation that seek to control and conform the church's way of life to their own desires and wishes. Or, it can be the work of confronting a dying congregation that a decision about its future can no longer be delayed. To be sure, there are many other forms this confrontation takes.

Regardless, confrontations in a congregation have two things in common. First, they require of the pastor and the congregation's leadership a shift in their beliefs, attitudes, and posture with regard to what it means to care. Simply put, confrontation is generally not associated with care because it brings dis-ease and disrupts settled ways of being. Moreover, confrontation smacks of judgment, and in fact, that's exactly what it is.

When one confronts the behavior or condition of another, she is making a judgment that that behavior or condition is adverse and destructive to the other's life and to the life of those around him. Conventional images of pastoral and spiritual care do not include images of judgment. Congregations call pastors to take care of them, not to confront or bring judgment upon them.

Secondly, congregations or individuals within congregations that receive the confrontation of a condition or detrimental behavior, and who take the long-term steps to change it—as opposed to finding a quick fix that will gloss over it—will always find the pathway to a life-giving future, even if that future means enduring the stresses of change or bringing their physical presence to a close.

Two of Jesus' most familiar sayings make clear that judgment and confrontation of conditions and behaviors are the pathways to freedom, and are in fact, essential components of love and care. One is the most loved passage, John 3:16, *"For God so loved the world that he gave his only Son, that whosoever believes will be saved."* For most, these words are understood to mean that God has overlooked our behavior, that he loves and accepts us just as we are. What is not read or heard are the words that follow in verses 19 and 20: *"And this is the judgment, that the light has come into the world, and people loved darkness rather than light because their deeds were evil."* Another way for the words of this text to be read might be, "For God so loved the world that he sent his Son that he brought judgment upon its condition and behaviors." In these words, judgment, love, and care are mutually inclusive of one another!

God's love includes bringing conditions and behaviors that stand in the way of life into the light. In John 8:32, Jesus declares, *"You shall know the truth, and the truth shall make you free..."* Consistent with John 3:16, these are not words that allow us to use God's love or belief in Jesus as an escape from destructive conditions or behaviors, but rather they open up the reality of how they have enslaved our lives and the lives of those around us. Paradoxically, we find our way to freedom and new beginnings! Thus, if the prophetic and priestly care of a congregation at its deepest levels is to reflect the love of the Spirit of the Holy One, it must include the work of confrontation, confronting the truths of conditions and behaviors that disrupt, detract or otherwise jeopardizes that congregation's ability to live out its vocational mission and work.

The following is the story of a congregation in which the pastor recognized the destructive behavior of one individual and its impact on the congregation's life and made the decision to confront it. It is the story of a pastor in a mid-size congregation and one of its influential members who attempted to intimidate him and the church's governing board. It is a moderate size congregation, but its immense structure and well-known music program make it a visible congregation in the community.

Prior to the pastor's coming, this member had lobbied to be appointed to the committee that would call the pastor. As he had done with the previous pastor, this person wanted to wield power, influence, and control over the pastoral office. He had been successful at doing this, due mostly to the preceding pastor's reluctance to challenge or confront him.

Not long after the current pastor's arrival, two board members began to receive abusive and threatening phone calls from the disgruntled member; and from the tone of his voice, they recognized his inebriated state. The phone calls were not isolated events; there were many. Upon receiving the report of these phone calls from the persons who received them, the pastor immediately recognized this to be a power he and the congregation's leadership would have to reckon with, not because it was a direct threat to him, but because it was interfering with the life of the congregation, and it was an attempt to sabotage the call and work of the congregation's elected leadership.

What differentiates this pastor's response from that of his predecessor's is that he does not attribute these incidents to the man's alcoholism. He does not give in to being sympathetic towards him as others had done. He recognized it as a power issue, that the man was trying to gain power over him and the elected leaders, just as he had done with previous pastors. In the past, the behavior of this person and been tolerated by pastors and the church's leadership out of sympathy for his problems with alcohol, but also because he happened to be the congregation's largest giver.

Deciding to confront the situation by bringing the matter to the governing board with a recommended plan of action, the pastor first initiated a conversation with the members' wife, who herself was a member of the governing board. In that meeting, the pastor laid before her the truth of her husband's behavior and the devastations it was causing, a truth of which she had long been in denial! Moreover, he directly told her his plan of bringing it before the governing board with a recommended plan of action. At the same time, he confronted her with the reality that he needed intervention and treatment.

Needless to say, she reacted vehemently, accusing him of being "un-Christian and un-caring." He held his ground, noting that he was only following the biblical admonition that these kinds of matters are to be taken to the ruling elders of the church. He did, in fact, follow through with his plan. The matter was taken to the governing board, and a letter was sent to the member, admonishing his behavior and insisting that he cease and desist his abusive behavior.

The matter was not resolved as we might hope. The member and his wife angrily left the congregation, apparently with no intent to seek help or address his drinking problem and the dysfunction it was causing. At the same time, however, their departure seemed not to create too much stir or reactivity among church leaders or congregants. More to the point, due to the pastor's decision and intervention, the congregation became unstuck from this person's behavior; its energies were now free to move forward with more constructive and life-giving endeavors.

We should not be so naive as to think this congregation is free from conflict. It is not! Conflict and disagreement are part of its nature. At the same time, and in large part due to the position the pastor took, its attitude towards conflict is different. Conflict remains, but it is less explosive, divisive power grabs are no longer present, and it seems more focused on pursuing a life-giving presence in its neighborhood and city. But what happens when a condition or reality has to do with the congregation's way of functioning in the face of an acute crisis or a chronic condition that has long existed within its "family" system? Such is the case in the present context of the pandemic, where the settled ways of life for many congregations have been severely disrupted, if not shut down altogether. For many, these disruptions have surfaced chronic conditions that long and adversely affected their ability to carry out a purposeful and missional vocation before Covid was even on the scene. The conditions and realities they face have confronted them with decisions to be made, and how they approach those decisions will have consequences for their ability to live into the future. The analogy I am about to use will seem strange and almost out of place, yet it is relevant.

Years ago, the head of the liver transplant team in the hospital where I worked said to a group of CPE students, "Transplants, regardless of the organ being transplanted, are not quick fixes; they are a complete change of life. If patients and their families cannot make the necessary changes to their life that the transplant requires, it will not be successful!"

The profound words of this physician could not be more applicable to the work with which congregations are faced when confronted with the crisis of facing their demise. Like persons facing life threatening illnesses that require transplants, the crises and truths with which congregations confronted are not inflicted by any one person; they are the result of changes taking place within their communities and neighborhoods, or within their own demographics. In either case, something has happened that the way of life they have had and known can no longer be sustained.

Confronted with this reality, congregations face the same choice as persons facing life changing decisions: they can remain in denial about what is happening and do nothing, or they can accept the truth and make changes that will open to them a new future and new possibilities. Quick fixes implemented with the goal of a hurried return to normal or a past way of life might provide immediate relief to the anxiety of the moment. However, they will not provide sustained life, nor will they open the congregation to a new future and new missional possibilities. Engaging the hard work of grief that comes with leaving behind the old and familiar, and the equally hard work of imagining a new identity and vision of themselves will generally lead a congregation into a new and life-giving future.

Two real-life and contrasting stories illustrate this point. First Church and Second Church are two congregations situated in the suburbs of a large metropolitan city. Both have had histories of being active and thriving congregations with missional foci. However, the communities and neighborhoods of each went through significant economic and demographic changes that impacted them, notably a dwindling of membership that in turn impacted their financial support and missional capabilities. At that point, their similarities end. Each faced the conditions and realities that confronted them with different attitudes and postures, hence different strategies.

First church was a congregation whose developing pastor had been with them for thirty years. Thanks to his leadership, it was a congregation with a strong missional history, including a corps of people who offered in-home assistance to AIDS patients. The pastor who succeeded him did not have this missional focus. The life of the congregation deteriorated from a worship attendance of 200 congregants to 40. To their credit, the congregation's leadership faced the stark reality that if the air conditioning failed, they literally would have no way to fix it. An interim pastor was brought in, but he, too, lacked vision and energy. The sick were not visited.

Eventually a new interim pastor was brought on and the very first thing she did was to visit every member of the congregation to hear their thoughts and feelings about their condition. Immediately after that visitation was completed, the congregation's leadership gathered for a retreat at which she directly confronted the leadership with what the congregation had told her in her visits. Notice that this confrontation was not her own assessment or speculation. It was a confrontation in which she placed in front of the leadership what the congregation had told her. It was clear that the congregation could no longer continue.

She took the confrontation one step further by saying directly that a decision about closing could no longer be deferred or delayed. Knowing this, she did not allow the leadership to waiver in its conversation. In fact, a decision was made at that same retreat, and steps were initiated to close the congregation. Her observation of that retreat was that it brought immense relief to both the leadership and the congregation's members. To her credit and the congregation's leadership, steps were taken to help congregants live into their end with grace and diminished anxiety. This included their legacy in the form of gifts to missional endeavors and going out together in groups to locate worshiping communities to which their members could relocate.

This does not mean that the work of leaving what is old for what is new came easy. To be sure it came with grief, disagreements, and anxiety. Yet they forged ahead because it created a future story that was hopeful. Using the language of care, we might say that this congregation cared so deeply for what it had been and what it could be, it was willing to let go of all that was old and familiar, yet no longer thriving, for something new that held the potential for life and life-giving mission, even if that future was not yet clear or defined!

The Second Church, on the other hand, was a contrasting story. While the congregation was aware of the conditions and realities, neither the pastor nor the leadership seemed stirred or concerned to confront or be confronted by what was happening. As one person described the situation "He (the pastor) saw his ministry as one of taking care of us without rocking the boat; and we were content to be taken care of and not have our boat rocked." As Ed Friedman so aptly describes, this is exactly what happens when leadership adapts to the organization's low threshold and tolerance for pain and anxiety and does not lead it to rise to the occasion to meet the challenges it faces. As we saw with the pastor and leadership confronting the destructive behavior of a member who was sabotaging their work, and as in the story of First Church, the willingness and ability of the pastor and leadership to increase its tolerance and threshold for anxiety, empowered the congregation to engage their conditions and realities and implement the changes they needed to make to leave what was old for what is new!

In the case of Second Church, a new pastor came after the old pastor left. She was called because it was believed she would provide an energy infusion into the congregation that would attract new and youthful members, all of which it was believed would pull the congregation out of its doldrums and downward spirals. In short, their way of "confronting" the truths and realities they faced was to find the quick fix, which, as it is for many congregations, was to find a youthful pastor who would bring in young members. The condition that had not yet been confronted was the reality that the congregation's way of life was not life-giving, and that life-giving behavior will not return because of a pastor's age or energy. It will only come from the spirit that others see and experience in the life of the whole congregation!

Like the young pastor called to Second Church, many pastors are caught in the trap of assuming responsibility to do exactly what the congregation wants: create new programs, create energy, work hard to bring in new members, etc. And then one day they wake up and realize they are tired, unfulfilled, and even depressed. They wake up to the fact that they have taken the emotional responsibility for whether or not the congregation lives into its future. Such is the case with the new pastor who came to Second Church. She awakened to the realization that she could not do for the congregation what it was unwilling to do for itself, that a shift in her ministry focus was required if she was to lead the congregation into new life and possibilities!

Perhaps the most challenging reality with which Second Church must be confronted is the axiom of which Ed Friedman so aptly reminds us: the changes required in order for us to meet the challenges in front of us are not external and "out there." Rather they are internal. The answer to Second Church's condition would not come from "infused energy," or a magical influx of new and youthful members. It could only begin with the internal work of redefining itself, redefining its vocational mission in light of its changing community and neighborhood, and defining what changes would be required within its own heart and soul to bring this new identity and vocation into reality. In contrast to First Church, this is not likely to happen because it has yet to take the risk of letting go of its old identity and re-imagining and re-envisioning a life-giving future, even if its physical presence no longer exists.

So, what might we gain from these three illustrations? I suggest the following:

>1. Confrontation in a congregation, regardless of the form it takes, is always an act of making judgment about a behavior or condition that is having an adverse effect on the congregation's ability to carry out its missional vocation. It is at the same time an act of deep love and care for the congregation and its life! The pastor confronting the behavior of the member knew what would happen if that behavior was not confronted. The pastor and leadership at First Church took the radical step of leading the congregation into radical changes, because they deeply cared about something beyond

the congregation's physical presence and its history—they cared about its missional vocation.

2. Confronting a congregation with disruptive behavior or conditions cannot be done by the pastor alone. It must include the congregation's leadership, as was done by the pastor confronting the member, and the pastor and leadership at First Church. At the same time, the non-anxious presence of the pastor will affect the kind of presence the leadership will have with the congregation, and in turn that presence will impact and empower the congregation's ability to approach its predicaments with lowered anxiety and increased confidence in its future. As we saw in Second Church, the church leadership's desire to seek quick fixes and easy answers served only to keep the congregation stuck in its desire to return to its past. While it was able to imagine ideas for how to attract new and younger members, it was not able to engage the work of re-imagining the internal work it would have to do to be a more welcoming, hospitable, and life-giving community.

3. The hoping process of a congregation—how it projects itself into the future—is integral to its ability to hear, receive, and engage truths and realities with which it is confronted. The pastor and leadership of the congregation that confronted the man with his intimidating and destructive behavior were able to transition from taking care of him and sympathizing with his destructive pathology,

because they were able to see that if such a confrontation did not take place, their immediate future would be more of the same—a life held captive to his intimidations and threats. Moreover, they were able to imagine a future where they would not be held captive to the idea that they needed his money in order to survive. They imagined themselves with new power! As much as they grieved their past, First Church was able to grieve and say good bye to what they had known, because their future story empowered them to see that as much as they might grieve it, what they had known did not hold the final word on who or what they could be in the community, even if their physical presence would be no more. Second Church's future story, on the other hand, is limited to its intent on resurrecting its past, which meant that it could not see a hopeful future unless that future was a return to its past. In this regard, it is a dysfunctional future story.

As difficult as it is, confrontation in a congregation that brings to light the conditions, behaviors, or devastations that keep it bound up and unable to live into its missional vocation will always hold the potential for it to change into more life-giving ways of functioning and living in community. Even when it hurts, makes the congregation angry, or makes people leave, the words of Jesus remain true, *"You shall know the truth and the truth will set you free!"*

Contact Info: Wayne Lee Menking, STD, Retired ACPE
Certified Educator, Fort Worth, TX
Wayne.Menking@acpe.edu

Chapter Sixteen:

Confrontation for Certification: Testing Personal and Professional Integration
by
Gordon J Hilsman

The phenomenon and art of confrontation is vital for the certification of chaplains, and even more so, in the certification of budding clinical pastoral educators. Both of these professions, in very different ways, require a degree of personal integration beyond what most professions require. To enter the arenas of human pain, spiritual belief and religious practice with people who are under considerable pressure and even alarm from illness, injury, or chronic conditions, not to mention the threat of dying, calls for significant knowledge, calming maturity, and facile and timely self-disclosure. Nobody is born with that kind of personal integration. It needs to be developed over time with practice, feedback from others, and experience. It is sustained then by a natural interest in the aspects of life that cannot be controlled or sometimes even influenced.[1]

There is a long history in the clinical ministry movement, of members who are intensely interested in the quality of spiritual care of deeply troubled people. One aspect of that history is how to decide who is ready to practice spiritual care in public institutions within the context of a pluralistic society. The story would be one of the "why" and "how" of certification and the primary criteria for that personal and professional integration.

In the twelve years I served on the national certification commissions for my professional organizations that certified clinical supervisors of spiritual care providers, the following scenario was very common. Five colleague reviewers would assemble with the applicant for certification as a supervisor (now called certified educators) for ninety minutes of communal exploration of the applicant's theory and theology of education, and their writing about their supervision of a chosen CPE group they had recently led. The meeting had been prepared for by a written presenter's report fashioned by one committee member summarizing the applicant's submitted writing about the details of CPE unit, and how they had supervised it.

The meeting would begin with the applicant using the written presenter's report to address the group. As the candidate talked about their supervision, the committee listened intently and quietly noted what they liked on the one hand and what they had questions about on the other. Typically, the candidate (we'll call them C) would describe a specific student and how they had assessed and supervised that student. Any committee member would draw attention to some incongruency or lacuna they had noticed, such as:

> M1: "I liked your writing. You describe things well and even colorfully. And I wondered how you

saw DD's (a member of their presented group) marked reticence to disclosure in the group."

C: "She was reticent. I wondered about that early on. But never was able to bring her very far into the fray."

M2: "Did you ever confront her habit of remaining peripheral to group interaction and individual supervision?"

C: "To some degree I did. Remember she has MS and seemed fragile most of the time. She never risked much in the group nor very deeply with me in individual supervision. But I thought she did enough with patients and staff, and some in the group, to qualify for credit."

N2: "I don't think you answered M2's question. How did you confront her reticence?"

C: "I guess I never did. Not sure why now that I think about it. Maybe she resembles somebody in my past."

N1: "What was there about her that kept you away from her emotionally?"

C: "Just her apparent vulnerability, I guess. I never really pressured her to participate."

Q: "How does your theory give you guidance in this complex situation? What does it tell you about supervising a student who frequently seems palpably vulnerable and communally reticent?"

C: "As I hear myself talking about this, I surmise Freud or some Freudian would wonder about transference, maybe reaction formation—you know, unconsciously doing the opposite of what you feel. Avoiding the intensity of your affect."

N1: "Do you mean in her or in you?"

C: "Wow. Both I guess."

Q: "How about educationally? What was your educational theory perspective on her?"

C: "My theory of education honors human boundaries fiercely. My primary published theorist says it's better to not do too much inviting of group members to participate because it tends to foster their continued dependence on you as a supervisor."

Thus, it would continue. The applicant talking seriously about themselves, their thinking about their presented students, their feelings about them, their learning about and from them, and how all that related to their stated, written theory of clinical pastoral education. The members of the certifying committee, all veteran educators interested in maintaining the high quality of clinical ministry, were quietly evaluating the *integration* of that candidate, seeking to convince themselves that the applicant was skilled and competent enough to have a supervisory perspective on almost any person they would accept into a clinical education program for the extent of a career. Was this applicant ready to be an autonomous practitioner developing, leading, and maintaining accredited clinical education programs in a variety of health care settings on a regular basis?

The purpose of certification is to authorize people to function as educators of caregivers in a given professional organization. The clinical ministry movement that began primarily in New England in the mid-1920s, injected new skills and identities of clergy caregivers into the care-giving world. As caregivers began to see strong emotions and subtle ones as the heart of the matter of care, they found they needed to invest much more in intentional awareness and understanding of their own emotions. The small group encounter milieu grew as educational experience for spiritual caregiving became real, stark, direct, and professionally intimate. Religious teaching in those situations and venues was reduced to only one, though major, component of care, as chaplaincy fostered interpersonal focus on a new kind of listening, to the inner experiences of troubled people. It was soon clear that such care required a new kind of preparation.

Real listening differs exponentially from the cognitive, academic, moral thinking approach that had dominated pastoral care up to that point. It was recognized that the changes needed to practice clinical spiritual (then called pastoral) education were *inside* those practitioners. They are fundamental. Everyone who aspires to a career as a clinical pastoral educator would need to change personally. The need to assess when educators were competent enough to practice as professionals, produced a new kind of certification process that featured considerable confrontation to get beneath the surface of a practitioners' practice. Over time, a unique culture developed in group certification of new educators (then called supervisors).

How to best assess competence is still an open question in my clinical spiritual education organizations, and I assume in other certifying bodies as well. One approach is to use the concept of integration as a somewhat observable yardstick.

There are essentially three kinds of personal integration needed. They still challenge anyone who takes clinical care of other people seriously as an endeavor and as a career. They are:

> 1. Cognitive/affective integration, necessary for authenticity and depth of care for the spirits of very troubled people.

> 2. Theory/practice integration, to determine whether an applicant tended to get stuck in either rationalized theory or ungrounded practice.

> 3. Integration of one's personal history into educational practice, forming a clinical educator identity.

Assessing Integration in Potential Clinical Pastoral Educators

Integration etymologically means "making one" (as in the emblem on U.S. coins—*e pluribus unum,* "from many, one"). The underlying theory is that most of us grow up with a conglomeration of quirks and defects to our personalities that serve as functional, and even interesting and colorful characteristics in ordinary conversations all our lives. However, such idiosyncrasies will often emerge as inconsistent and ineffective in a professional practice that clinically educates highly diverse academically educated religious leaders, charged with caring for human spirits in public institutions of a pluralistic society. Those troubling idiosyncrasies will likely be exposed within the context of personal encounter in experiential education in small process groups of group clinical supervision. There is no simple way to do that. But the process will include careful, powerful confrontation.

Clinical spiritual care and education is best led by an educator who functions with a degree of professional integration, which includes, even presupposes, a fair amount of personal integration. A group leader can be straightforward with the group and each of its members, to the degree that that educator can be open, clear, and congruent in the crucial moment. Certification asks, "Can this applicant for certification say what they mean, mean what they say, and not say too much. Can they do so with consistency, authenticity, sensitivity, and an adequate use of various approaches based on the personalities and previous experience of very diverse students? That identity and practice stretches every applicant, no matter their previous education and life experience.

An entire book could be written on this unique method of assessing integration through a variety of interventions. At great risk of being reductive, one way of organizing the process of assessing integration in certification is to confront supervisory students in the moment regarding their affect, cognition, behavior, and communication all in the same conversation. Can they talk clearly about what they think about a student, how they are feeling immediately about the student's care efforts, and what they remember having done in that attempt to carefully educate. In ACPE certification history, there have developed questions that can serve as examples of interventions that manifest either *adequate competence* or need for further education as outcomes of the certification meeting, i.e. certification or denial of certification. All are necessarily confrontative.

1. Cognitive/Affective Integration

Integration of one's *thinking, emotions,* and *active behavioral choices* ordinarily develops mostly in highly emotionally charged situations that require vigorous use of several interpersonal functions, in such arenas as psychotherapy, grieving major losses, falling in love, and confrontation in group process work, such as clinical pastoral education. We don't smoothly evolve our integration, but rather are shaken into it by unavoidable circumstances, uncontrollable events, and overwhelm, in combination with the personal and interpersonal help we get in the midst of the chaos those emotionally charged situations can precipitate. Our personality adaptations to the painful historical aspects of our life experience are just too strong to go away simply because we recognize them and want to rid ourselves of them. We need solid and caring confrontation to pull the disparate aspects of our personalities together into a relatively congruent whole. Clinical pastoral education itself and certification events tend to contribute to that process.

In the certification context, certifiers are asking themselves, "Can this applicant talk about their emotions about a student in vignettes, distinguishing between the basic emotions of anger, sadness, hurt, fear, joy, and regret (guilt/shame). And can they switch with some facility and apparent authenticity to their thinking about that same student. A few examples of many questions and immediate direct observations typically used during that one ninety-minute certification meeting may be:

- How did you feel in general about them (a specific student)?

- How were you feeling when they said/did that (a specific response or event)?

- What were you feeling besides annoyed? (Hurt? Fear? Sadness? Shame?...)

- What do you think was behind your excessive anger at that point/student? (transference, projection, rationalization, justifying?)

- It seems like you're getting a bit riled right now.

- You seem to be withdrawing emotionally from this committee right now.

2. Theory/Practice Integration

The flexibility of a clinical supervisor to shift focus from concrete descriptions of a student to theoretical conceptualizations allows them to better decide how to supervise that student. Certification tests whether an applicant has done enough serious talking about students to begin working as an educator with that flexibility to carry a nimble presence in group supervision. Getting stuck in principles makes one pedantic, dampening, and boring in the group. And it prevents learning "in the moment." On the other hand, getting stuck in immediate observations of group dynamics, robs group members of the opportunity to learn concepts that make conversing about caring relationships more efficient and communicable. Identifying adequate flexibility in switching between these two perspectives convinces a certification group that an applicant's theory is really a theory—*a collection of intertwining principles that gives direction in situations of great complexity*—and that that theory is really theirs in practice, not merely a series of rationalizations in order to get certified.

Some certification confrontations that test the relative integration between theory and practice of a candidate for certification can be, for example:

- I hear your description of DS in that vignette. What aspects of your theory serve you in supervising them?

- I hear your theoretical assessment of DS. Can you give an example of how you actually used that theory in supervising them?

- What do you mean in your theory by the term (any concept, from ego to grace)?

- When your primary theory fails to address group issues, as with JK, what secondary theory of group dynamics serves you?

3. Integration of One's Personal History into Educational Practice Forming a Clinical Educator Identity

Early clinical educators noted that a person who was validated by a group of peers for functioning relatively consistently as an authentic caregiver, and could talk about themselves and their care relationships clearly, seemed to have become personally different. Their convincing new confidence was recognized as a new identity, as if there was a new person inside them. Early Christians called that same phenomenon "putting on Christ." Military people grasp the phrase, "Once a soldier always a soldier," and physicians know when a person does not just "impersonate a doctor" but actually is one. Those early educators called it a "pastoral identity," when they saw it in a developing student and could count on that student to care for most any deeply troubled person genuinely and skillfully to whom they were assigned to care. One component of that identity is extensive experience of having been confronted repeatedly about their care efforts enough to gain that confidence-combined-with-competence that constitutes a new identity.

Competence without confidence remains reticent, fledgling, and maybe courageously trying. Confidence without competence is mere bravado and theater (playing church is the old term), and can be dangerous when officially authorized to practice as a professional. The two together can be seen as a solid pastoral identity.

At least two things are different in that new person: humility, i.e. a self-understanding that knows and accepts both one's own gifts and limitations, and a clinical perspective on care.

Clinical in this context refers to *an approach to helping people that features direct observation, objective discernment, and use of established but evolving frameworks of understanding people, relationships, and their human interactions.* Clinical education is designed to develop a caregiver's trust of their own direct observations and impressions of people's difficulties, combined with some conceptual language of psychology, theology, and other helping disciplines that facilitate professional dialogue about those difficulties. Clinical spiritual care proceeds from a place of one's own direct observation rather than pervasive belief, narrow religious conviction, or pop psychology. Medicine and spiritual care are being increasingly reshaped to work together in such integrative caregiving efforts as palliative care, addiction recovery, professional chaplaincy, and spiritually informed psychotherapy. All of them rely on empathic confrontation as key interventions in their care.

A professional identity in this context is shaped by a supervisory candidate's being sufficiently confronted on how their own personal history affects their relationships with students to allow them to maintain as objective perspective as possible in their educational work. Reflecting on one's reactions to specific students and how one feels in various situations with them, gradually forms the new identity, that of supervisor, on top of the chaplain identity that was developed in chaplaincy education. This is especially true when a budding educator has strong emotions that seem out of proportion to what one might expect in a specific interaction. Tracing those emotions and impulsive actions to one's personal history often enough informs an educator about how to intervene more helpfully to various educational opportunity moments with peers and students.

A small group arena works best for this, because it allows direct feedback from several peers at once to help one another see themselves more as patients see them, than relying on their own impressions only. Learning how to use this powerful group confrontation is a primary early learning of chaplaincy students and becomes even more crucial in forming a supervisory identity for leading and managing programs of clinical education.

The professional certification interview is essentially a testing of whether a person has learned from being confronted enough to be allowed to officially confront others in person and in the writing of official student evaluations that will persist in files to verify clinical education competence. The ability to confront others with piercing accuracy, perspicacious timing, courageous initiative, and deep empathy still stands as a fundamental skill in the certification of both chaplains and clinical spiritual educators.

4. Therapy/Education Distinction

Besides these aspects of integration, certifiers of clinical educators are accustomed to test the applicant's distinction between clinical education and therapy or counseling. It takes deft confrontation after careful observation to make this determination in a few certification minutes. Does this applicant for certification keep the sometimes-blurry lines as clear as possible between therapy and education? There seems to be a strong temptation on the part of budding educators to practice group therapy rather than group clinical education.

Therapy in this context means *helping another person recognize and heal aspects of their personality and relational functioning to improve the success and satisfaction of their lives.* Clinical education here is *helping caregivers to improve their care relationships through actual experience of caring for people and communal reflection on that improving care.* Put simply, the one is about getting help for oneself, the other about helping people improve their care of others. Even when an applicant has incorporated that distinction into their theory, there is still a tendency to engage too vigorously in curative interventions in the group, instead of recognizing and referring them to counseling or therapy. Some certification interventions intended to confront the slide into therapy can be, for example:

- "It seems like you lost sight for a time, of the educational goals of student CW. What was the primary goal of your own that seemed so important?" (Of course, sometimes the goal of an educator for a student *is* more fitting than the student's own particular goal).

- "How did you deal with WG's current and historical indicators of a drinking problem/co-dependence?"

- "Are you satisfied with how you met GR's apparent OCD 'freezing' in that second week group?"

- "How did you feel during BG's rage event in that pivotal group session?"

On occasion it becomes prescriptive to ask an applicant for distinctions between their definitions of therapy, education, and consultation vs. certification, as well. Keeping these clear in one's mind can be a milestone in becoming a clinical educator.

Clinical education *as a chaplain* is transformative for those who choose to engage and even embrace it in supervised group education. Training formation for a career of supervising, organizing, and maintaining that kind of experiential group education is even more shaking and transformative. Weak education as an educator has great potential to do harm to students, if they are prematurely certified, as well as dilute the depth of their clinical supervision for their career. If they then find their way onto certification committees, the process of diminishing the entire field ensues. It takes considerable care to make the decisions of a person's readiness for such a career in certification meetings. Sorting the capacity of applicants for both certification as chaplains on the one hand, and as clinical pastoral educators on the other, will only be done with consistent, persistent confrontation by those who have gone before. And it is extremely sensitive, intricate, and important work.

5. Confrontation for Certification of Chaplains

The process for certification of chaplains has been patterned after the one for educators which preceded it. It contains core elements of the educator certification process, but differs significantly in intensity, scope, and tone. It tends to be much less confrontative, while preparing applicants for a very different profession. A primary goal of the processes for certification in the APC, NACC, NAJC, and the Canadian CASC remains use of confrontation adequate to assess shared sets of competencies for chaplaincy, and to thus maintain the quality of clinical ministry by well-integrated chaplains in North America. What makes the practice of clinical pastoral care of patients and parishioners so unique is its vigorous mingling of cognition with strong and obvious or subtly discernable emotion.

    Chaplain education serves as the arena for engaging would-be pastoral care professionals, because its programs are set in places where there are people experiencing the worst of life. Invariably health care patients, jail/prison inmates, hospice residents, and mental health patients feel deeply about fundamental aspects of their life situations. From ordinary daily apprehensions and annoyances, persons in such situations often escalate to cold, secretive fear, deep remorse, nagging hurt, and/or aggravating rage. A great number of them could use help with those feelings that can become overwhelming, at least temporarily. The behavioral sciences have made great progress in the past 150 years in care of those most troubled spirits. Chaplaincy provides a vital link to those other professions, as often the first to identify serious, painful personal, interpersonal, and communal issues. Excellent chaplaincy sensitively refers them and takes referrals from them, partnering in team treatment providing unique, trusted to be positive, and extensive personal listening.

Chaplain certification—*authorization to practice professional chaplaincy*—is a small group testing out one's practice, as seen through the windows of stated competencies considered necessary for chaplaincy. The certifiers are optimally looking and listening for integration, a "making one" of several human functions of an applicant for certification—and for the applicant to do so well enough to be able to address the tasks of clinical spiritual care effectively in relationship with most every patient presented before them.

Some contexts starkly invite the responsibility for furthering human integration, though we can certainly reject the challenge. We are occasionally pulled into some of the most effective arenas for doing that, such as: psychotherapy when motivated by genuine pain; major loss when repeatedly conveyed to another through courageous, extensive narrative; clinical supervision and mentoring, when it is allowed to absorb us; carried-away romantic engagement and its subsequent intimate loving foray; and the vividly recognized approach of one's own dying. All of these are examples of situations that cast us into choosing change that both hurts and promises.

The capacity to meet a crucial patient encounter with authenticity means: conveying empathy about some aspect of the patient's predicament; saying only what you mean but clearly saying it; allowing what you actually feel to significantly affect you in being responsive but not reactive; acknowledging those feelings as real and just fine, but not necessarily processed with the patient; believing in your current thinking about the patient and augmenting it with listening and careful questions and observations; and recognizing the implications of a unique care moment and embracing them, attributing positive intent to that patient. All of these combined—thoughts, feelings, words, meanings, attitudes, and choices working together constitute personal integration. It is what is being sought, to an always unnamed degree, or ought to be, during a chaplaincy certification event. When someone pins on a badge that blares "Chaplain," it ought to mean that the person wearing it carries a well-developed identity born of experience and enough personal integration events to render them consistently available to virtually any other person on the planet for authentic healing engagement. While no one is ever totally integrated—we live in incomplete evolution—true professionals know that a significant level of integration, which can only be subjectively assessed, is required for practicing their craft.

Certification interview teams are looking for a level of integration that will allow consistent authenticity in professional practice. *Lack of it* is more observable than *its possession*. Super nice compliance; unacknowledged contentiousness; subtle victim stances; inability to exemplify concepts or to conceptualize about events; humorless stridency; confusing verbosity; extensive nervous monologues; inability to see the interviewers as real people; these are all indicators, (and only indicators) to certifiers, that adequate integration was not able to be mustered in that moment. They do not mean the applicant is a lesser human being or even that they are not functioning as a fine chaplain with many of the people they care for.

6. Integration Demonstrated

There are also indicators that integration *is* being demonstrated. When interviewers encounter an applicant, a few hints that significant personal integration is being demonstrated include:

- Calm acknowledgement of the emotions, sometimes conflicting, that flow through one's reverie at any given time

- Ease of movement between head and heart— between what one thinks and what one feels

- Accurate use of a few concepts—existential (descriptive), psychological, psychosocial, personality theory, human development, or theological—in discussing patients and family members.

- Apparent awareness and acknowledgement of one's own motivation and attitudes, with minimal defensiveness

- Articulation of one's own values, with examples of how they motivate actions and the pursuit of life decisions and directions (and a personal or professional failure or two as well)

- Speaking specifically about one's own painful life events with perspective, insight and emotional freshness, rather than bravado, hyperbole, signs of shame, hints of resentment, or subtle victim tones

- Immediate use of enjoyable situational humor, imagination, and creativity that is not cynical, avoidant, and nervously contrived

Becoming a certifier in a professional organization is no small undertaking. It often requires astute observation and concise, prescriptive confrontation. That role holds careers in one's hands. It ought to be a seasoned chaplain or educator who agrees to take on that role, or is ever officially invited to do so.

[1] Gordon J. Hilsman, *Spiritual Care in Common Terms—How chaplains can effectively describe the spiritual needs of patients in medical records,* (Philadelphia: Kingsley, 2017).

Chapter Seventeen

Confronting God: Passionately Addressing the Power Beyond Us All
by
Gordon J Hilsman

"When you wish upon a star, makes no difference who you are, anything that you desire will come to you."

There is a positive value to magical thinking at times, especially for children to incorporate a positive attitude about the world in their development. One of the places it finds its limits however, is in healthcare where it so often fails and leaves people abandoned and discouraged.

As a Catholic school boy, I learned that there are four types of prayer, and I have since been convinced by an activist to add one more. All of them, to be of a quality to enhance the human spirit, need certain characteristics. They sometimes need to be confrontive, or authentically intimate, reaching from the core of the person praying. They are best when emotionally expressive, but valuable just in finding the fitting words for expression. That is eloquence. Published prayers can help with that. Or they can deaden it.

I learned something lasting with one of my very first prayers with a patient in a hospital setting. I was visiting preoperative people mixed together in a large urban medical center. I was already a priest and also a student in a CPE program, my first in a hospital setting. One man got my attention with the look on his face, concerned, stressed, and almost pleading. Failing to engage him successfully, I told him I would say the Lord's Prayer with him. He nodded and I took his hand, said the words of the prayer slowly, sat for a moment, and left the room.

The next day I at another room to visit people post-op. As I entered the room, the same man raised up, spoke with enthusiasm to his roommate, telling him, "There he is, there he is, the one I told you about. He was here with me yesterday and prayed."

You can never tell who may be moved by your prayer. And rote prayers can be unpredictably powerful at times.

Still, spontaneous prayer that is real and engaging of the inner concerns of a patient, adds to and can exceed the connectedness of the isolated person by injecting the feeling of being connected also to the Divine, called by any name. Most experienced chaplains know that the crying most often occurs during the prayer, whether during or after the human encounter.

Back in grade school we were taught these ways of praying:

1. Praise or Adoration

The euphoric practice of singing about the greatness of God or Jesus, encountering the Creator in the natural world, and the intentional expression of appreciation of the beauty of humanity, romance, sexuality and children is found in praise and adoration. It can be a momentary realization of present beauty or a patterned communal practice led by a religious official on a regular basis. It is being jolted out of our ordinary stream of consciousness to speak the extraordinariness underneath it. It often takes intentional effort and tends to leave residual joy about the world for at least a brief time, regardless of circumstances. If you've done this with genuine feeling at church, you will feel it on the way home.

2. Gratefulness

Akin to adoration, is the buoyant experience of happenings that please us, such that we express it directly to the Divine, the assumed Creator of everything we know, whether we see that as personal or impersonal. It is more an experience than an obligation but can be felt in shame when emphasized by another person's teaching that it is a duty. It comes upon us as we enjoy the world and can't stop ourselves from finding something or someone to thank, as in skiing down a mountain, before or after eating, people gathered for shared experience.

In spiritual care, a prayer of gratefulness increases good feelings about the positive side of difficult medical conditions, situations, or happenings. It can gather together reasons for being thankful at times when summation of a life fits the situation, such as near death, after the birth of a related infant, or the wedding of offspring.

3. Regret, Sorrow

An expression of inner hurtful sadness about something in the past, especially our own imperfect or atrocious behavior, brings about regret and sorrow. Prayer of regret is essentially a felt, expressed apology, bringing into verbal processing our negative feelings about pain we may have caused others, our own person, or humanity in general by contributing to its ills. In Catholic practice, it is always a part of the sacrament of confession, and in a pinch, supplants it. Confession as a spiritual skill is now more obviously alive in the fifth of the Twelve Steps: "Admitted to God, ourselves and another human being, the exact nature of our wrongs." [1]

In hospitalized people and also the imprisoned, the adolescent, and the addicted in any stage of recovery, imputing regret to the subject as we pray for them, bridges a gap between internal regret and external reticence to address the Divine. The words, Forgive NAME for anything he/she has ever done that they regret, can fall as soft rain to a dry soul on a scorching day.

4. Petition

The human impulse to ask for what is your dire need, or even your legitimate want, was not lost on Jesus or other spiritual leaders who suggested it. It has often been said that the most difficult thing we do is find out what we really want, because we will eventually get it in some way. Putting forth your most conscious, especially urgent desire, helps clarify what it is we really want, beyond the surface of retail flash. But experience tells us that we can't get what we want by praying for it. Ask the boy who prays for all he's worth to stop wetting the bed, the farmer who desperately needs rain to save the farm, and the pediatric parent who sees the life of their daughter slowly slipping away.

Excellent prayer of petition follows the example of Jesus in the Garden the night before his torture and death. In effect, "I don't want this. I hate this. But Father if you want this for me, okay. Thy will be done." Prayer of petition must make room for a prayer of acceptance. There is still too much cause for unbearable pain in this unfinished, evolutionary world.

5. Protest

In recent years, one of my colleagues suggested, urged, insisted, that there is another form of prayer that is even more confrontational. That is expressing to the ubiquitous Power Beyond Us All, that we just don't like what is happening, how it is organized, how slow it takes to improve, who is in charge of horrible systems, and that people still die way too early in life. That kind of prayer is heard in the mourning of grieving women is some cultures, sometimes even paid for providing that context for grieving. Viscerally expressing our protest at what we see as outrageous evil—torture, rape, combat, not to mention bullying, domestic violence, public calumny—won't make it go away. But it can make it momentarily bearable, as we trudge on yearning and working for a more just world. Job showed the way, unrequited in the original ending.[2]

[1] Al-Anon Family Group Head Inc., *From Paths to Recover—Al-Anon's Steps, Traditions and Concepts—Step 5,* (Virginia Beach, Al-Anon Family Group Headquarters: 1997), 53-56.

[2] Book of Job, all of chapter 37.

EPILOGUE ONE

Five Confrontations I've Needed in My Lifetime that Never Came
by
Gordon J Hilsman

One sees more in aging years than earlier in the life cycle. In the mid-twentieth century not much seemed to be known by the public about risking confrontation, when now, looking back, the need for confrontation even in friendship may seem obvious to some. Getting what, in retrospect, I believe would have helped me make fewer poor life choices would have taken a prophet of some sort, or a very interpersonally advanced person to see, reflect on, and risk caring enough to say what they saw that I needed to hear. But these examples suggest how we as a human race could do better for one another, if the skills and virtues of caring confrontation were widely practiced, may point us to directions to continue evolving this treasured kind of communication. We are evolving in this direction it seems, so why not attempt to enhance that process with our careful observation and courageous use of what we see to help one another better develop as part of this great human race. It would be a great contribution to overcoming the brutal criticism that pervades some social media venues, classrooms, teams, entertainment venues, and even politics. Confronting rather than dominating, criticizing, and ridiculing must be a goal of our generation and the ones that follow.

1. Ball Hog

As a senior in a small Catholic high school, I was the most athletic in my class—one of the best basketball players in the school. We had four very good basketball players. Two tall juniors and a very athletic sophomore, who would eventually be the best of us all. We had several mediocre players that could fill out the first five. But we only won three games that year. We had no experienced coach. The nice man history teacher, who organized us, had never played the game. He couldn't coach any of us at any position, nor help us work together as a team—at all. The confrontation I needed desperately from someone, anyone, was along these lines:

> "Gees Gordon! You have got to learn a few things about this game. You have a 6'3" center (Bill) who can dunk the ball, (rare at the time, 1959), has a great hook shot, and can move like a guard. GET THE BALL TO HIM! Learn how to pass, think about him as you bring the ball down on offense, work at making him successful, even great. Pass to Larry, and Ray to pass to Bill. You take way too many shots, from anywhere and everywhere, and still average only 14 points a game. You could easily be

called a ball hog, a hot dog, a self-centered kid! Get ahold of yourself on the court."

I'm sorry Bill, Ray and Larry, wherever you are.

2. Wrong Major

I majored in Chemistry in college. What a mistake. It didn't fit me. I got an A in literature, psychology, and religion in that fine, small Catholic college. But I struggled continually with every course in physics and chemistry to qualify for my major and minor. I was in a seminary section of the college, and I spent time running on the cross-country team and playing on basketball teams, science classes, and studying, not on broadening my life with relationships and clubs. It should have become obvious, that I was out of my element in the math aspects of any science major. But my counselor was the chair of the chemistry department and nobody saw the mistake I was making in what to study. At least nobody said it. I needed somebody to confront me about that, as in:

> "Gees Gordon. Are you sure you're on the right track here? It's the end of your sophomore year and you're barely making it in science, but get A's in lit and psychology. Why waste your time in the chem lab and library carrels buried in stuff you don't even understand. Maybe you should try writing about people and the weird things that make them tick. You'll never be a chemist and don't even want to be. Do something you enjoy, that excites you, and follow that."

I think I might have gotten my head out of my rear and gotten a better fit, if I had heard something like that a lot earlier in life.

3. Buried Emotions

Shortly after ordination, three friends and I were headed to a party about eighty miles away. Two were twins who had pilot's licenses and a Dodge Charger with a big engine, a straight transmission, and no frills to use of energy on anything but driving the wheels. One of us offered a bet, that the car could beat the plane to the party, including getting to one airport and back from the other. My friend Tom and I took the car. We thought we had a good chance to beat the airplane. Tom drove first and got that car up over a 117 mph on the narrow treacherous highways of rural Iowa. I got it up to 131. At that rate, if we'd hit a twig on the highway, it may have been the end of us. I don't even remember who won the bet, but it was close. Gripping that steering wheel tensed and inflexible, stubborn and clueless, should have been a hint at the way I was typically dealing with my observations and feelings. I needed somebody to notice that and confront me, as in:

> "Gees Gordon. That was crazy. You were seconds from death for over an hour. For what? You put yourself there. Wasn't there a moment when that dawned on you? Maybe you should look at what celibacy does to some guys. You have to dull your real feelings to continue living the vow. Lots of

priests live stunted lives because of that, more like bachelors than celibates. You grew up mostly ignoring your emotions, or minimizing them, or bending them, or intentionally hiding them, making them secondary to your thick mind. Are you still doing that?" It took me ten more years to take action on that advice I needed, but that never came.

4. Lagging Integrity

After I was certified as an acting supervisor in the ACPE at the age of 34 and still a Catholic priest, I got romantically involved with a crazy fun woman my age, who lived in a town twenty miles away. I lived that way for over a year. I'd be gone from the rectory at odd hours, sometimes overnight, so the three priests who lived there too must have at least suspected. When I finally decided to leave the priestly ministry, a good friend of mine who had written a book called, *The Sexual Celibate,* suggested I find a way to be both a celibate priest and be sexually active with somebody I loved. I said, "Ben, I've got to get some integrity back into my life." For well over a year, I needed somebody to confront me with something like:

> "Gees Gordon. How can you do this? Time will reveal a little of how many people you are hurting with this secret scandal, and how much. This adolescent behavior will all come out eventually. Many people are charmed by your quirky, human-to-human, guitar-singing,

gimmicky, sharp wisdom sermons. But where is your integrity? You're posturing like a celibate and living like a bachelor. Sure, no matter what you do—celibate priest or married father—you will grieve deeply the loss of the other life. And it will be the most difficult decision you'll ever make—it was. But eventually, you'll have to choose one or the other. Meanwhile, you're eroding your soul with this bullshit; for God's sake get in or get out!"

5. Painful Neglect

Nancy and I had three children: Ashley, Simon and Brady, all within three and a half years. I worked as a chaplain at the local small-town hospital and a fine alcoholism treatment facility. I started a CPE program, maintained an old house with three quarters of an acre yard, heated with wood, finished a doctorate, and dedicated a lot of time to the ACPE for certification committee work and as regional treasurer. I neglected my kids. I couldn't see it until I was in my mid-sixties, when it was impressed upon me by my exceptional nurse daughter to look at it. I needed someone, anyone, to confront me a lot earlier about my daily life choices, like:

> "Gees Gordon, look at yourself. Your kids need you and you all but ignore them with your work preoccupation. They love you, so they won't tell you, but they yearn for time with you—fishing, boating, camping, watching silly movies with

you, watching their sports games, teaching what you do know about everything, setting their personalities for an enjoyable, loving, and successful life. Each of them NEEDS YOUR UNDIVIDED ATTENTION FOR FIFTEEN MINUTES ALMOST EVERY DAY!!! Your wife sees them and spends time with them, thank God for that. But they need their father, in their faces, and this is the best time of your life, too. You're missing it!"

Who could have said that? Nobody at that time. But we are evolving into a human race where people will courageously say things like that out of loving care. Soon, I hope.

(I'm sorry Ashley, Simon and Brady. But you've heard that before. Doesn't help much does it?)

There is a Catholic tradition called the "spiritual works of mercy." One of them is "admonish the sinner", meaning seeing what a person is doing that is hurting self, others or the community, and confronting them about it. We still need that "going against" in our society, (but maybe in different words?). We must believe that the skills, attitudes, courage and care it takes is growing, as we evolve.

EPILOGUE TWO

Skills Not Easily Learned
by
Sandra Walker

As a Clinical Pastoral Education intern and the recipient of challenging feedback, I was both repelled and intrigued. My overly honed ego was initially bruised when after presenting an "airtight" verbatim in my first unit of CPE, my old-school supervisor suggested we all go home since Sandy didn't seem to have anything to learn.

In fact, until that first unit, I *didn't* think I had much to learn. When subsequent verbatims were red inked in comments like, "You moved away, you missed the patient, you need to move your visits to levels of greater depth and intimacy," I saw how I could get better at this work and I was hooked. Not that I was always receptive. A few years later during my CPE residency, my supervisor said I often came across in the peer group like I had all the right answers. "You have to admit," I said, "that I am right most of the time." Then I quoted him my favorite line from the movie Broadcast News, when the character played by Holly Hunter is confronted by her boss who sarcastically remarks, "Wow, it must feel great to be the only person in the room who's right." She hilariously responds, "No. It's just awful."

My kindly supervisor nevertheless suggested that I might benefit from holding my assumptions a bit more lightly and checking out my intuition with others. By the end of the year, he and the group got through to me—no doubt sparing me years of professional embarrassment and heartache.

So, while the giving and receiving of direct confrontation did not come quickly to me, it has been life-changing both personally and professionally. Moreover, I have witnessed the benefits of astute feedback on patients as a chaplain, to students as their clinical educator, in cohort groups following peer-to-peer confrontation, and in certification interviews. Done well and within the context of empathic, caring relationships, confrontation can be transformative for the recipient. At the same time, *there is no guarantee that we will consistently get it right*. I know this experientially and intrinsically, as I have unintentionally wounded others with an impulsive comment or overly harsh critique and have run roughshod over another's healthy defenses. Conversely, I have lost the plot in a haze of niceties and the camouflage of kindness.

Even when done well, the recipient of a well-thought-out, insightful confrontation may respond with defensiveness, anger, or hurt. Confrontation within the context of professional, pastoral, and educational relationships is an art. Becoming effective and fluent in this art has been the subject of this book.

Contact Info: Sandra Walker, MDiv, Co-Editor, ACPE Certified Educator, Providence Portland Medical Center, Portland OR   Sandra.Walker@providence.org

OTHER BOOKS BY GORDON J. HILSMAN

Available on Amazon

Intimate Spirituality: The Catholic Way of Love and Sex (2007), Gordon J. Hilsman presents sexual loving as integral to rather than separate from most people's spiritual lives. His coalescing of intimate love with traditional Catholic concepts—virtues, capital sins, fruits of the Spirit, sacraments—augments the pervasively moral view of sex with a spiritual perspective that highlights its beauty and power to shape the virtue of people's lives. Seeing sexual attraction as built into humanity by the Creator to feed and challenge virtually all persons worldwide, he illustrates how intimate loving is actually a neglected aspect of Christian spirituality that has never been developed as fully as the individual and the communal. Hilsman calls upon theologians and spiritual leaders to further develop the understanding of intimate loving as a genuinely beautiful spiritual aspect of life.

Spiritual Care in Common Terms: How Chaplains Can Effectively Describe the Spiritual Needs of Patients in Medical Records (2017), Encouraging a broad, compassionate, humanistic approach to spirituality, this book shows how patients' spiritual needs can be communicated well within interdisciplinary teams, leading to better patient wellbeing.

This book describes the art of charting patients' spiritual perspectives in an open way that will help physicians and nurses to better direct medical care. It includes practical information on how to distil spiritual needs into pragmatic language, helping to demystify spiritual experience. Drawing on his extensive practical experience, the author also suggests key points to emphasize that will enrich chart notes for medical records, including brief, relative narratives, trusting one's own impressions, reflecting holistically on the patient's life, patient attitudes towards treatment and recovery, and describing families' opinions on the health care situation of their loved one. The book shows healthcare professionals of all disciplines how to engage in a shared responsibility for the spiritual care of their patients.

How to Get the Most Out of Clinical Pastoral Education: A CPE Primer (2018), This accessible primer sets out the core elements and methods of Clinical Pastoral Education (CPE), and shows how to use it most effectively to improve clinicians' capacity for spiritual care.

The guide explains how to learn best from verbatim sessions, open agenda groups and writing projects. It shows how the primary learning modalities of CPE add competence to a spiritual caregiver's practice, suggesting helpful ways to reflect on spiritual care encounters from varying perspectives. It recommends ways to collaborate with a peer group, enhance frameworks of understanding people, improve self-awareness and broaden one's scope of caring while also deepening it. Written by an experienced supervisor of the Association for Clinical Pastoral Education, this guide is an essential introduction for anyone seeking to foster positive attitudes and practice of spiritual care in hospitals, hospices and other clinical settings.

Made in United States
Orlando, FL
04 May 2022